BAPTISM AND MINISTRY

LITURGICAL STUDIES, ONE

Ruth A. Meyers, Editor,
for the Standing Liturgical Commission

The Church Hymnal Corporation
New York

D1069444

Preface

Liturgical Studies are collections of essays issued from time to time under the direction of the Standing Liturgical Commission. They reflect the fact that our liturgical prayer, while formally set forth in The Book of Common Prayer and other authorized books and collections of texts, is also continually developing and unfolding as it becomes the experience of Christians continuing week by week "in the apostles' teaching and fellowship, in the breaking of bread, and in the prayers."

To encounter the risen Christ in common prayer is often to find ourselves confronted by questions and new perceptions which arise out of the very act of worship itself. It is these questions and new perceptions which are the subject matter of Liturgical Studies.

These essays are offered as a stimulus to thought, reflection and further discussion. It is the hope of the Standing Liturgical Commission that they will be seen as a contribution to an ongoing conversation born out of our experience of worship in the Anglican tradition. The essays do not necessarily reflect the views of the Standing Liturgical Commission, and in some cases a particular essay may be at variance with another essay in the same collection.

We welcome your responses to the essays and see them as a way of expanding the conversation as well as helping the Commission to carry out its canonical mandate "to collect and collate material bearing upon further revisions of The Book of Common Prayer."

The Rt. Rev. Frank T. Griswold
Chair, Standing Liturgical Commission

Introduction

In the course of just a few decades, the Episcopal Church has undergone a radical change in its theology and practice of Christian initiation. With the 1979 Book of Common Prayer, a new pattern of initiation into the Christian faith has become normative in the Episcopal Church. In earlier Prayer Books, confirmation was requisite for admission to communion and so could be understood as the completion of Christian initiation. But the 1979 Prayer Book defines baptism as "full initiation by water and the Holy Spirit into Christ's Body the Church."[1]

In most congregations, the practice of private baptism on Sunday afternoon, attended by family and a few friends, has been replaced by the celebration of Baptism as the chief service of the congregation on Sundays or other feasts. Many parishes reserve baptisms for the occasions recommended by the Prayer Book: the Easter Vigil, the Day of Pentecost, All Saints' Day or the Sunday after All Saints' Day, the Feast of the Baptism of our Lord (the First Sunday after the Epiphany), and a bishop's visitation.[2] Baptism is increasingly a joyous celebration involving an entire congregation, rather than a private family affair celebrating the birth of a child.

The "confirmation rubric," restricting communion to those confirmed (or "ready and desirous" of being confirmed), has been eliminated, permitting communion of all the baptized. In some places infants are admitted to communion at the time of their baptism, a practice affirmed by the House of Bishops in 1988.

Confirmation remains as a rite of mature profession of faith for those baptized as infants. But the Prayer Book rite of "Confirmation with forms for Reception and for the Reaffirmation of Baptismal Vows" also allows individual Christians to reaffirm their faith at other significant moments in their lives. Many Episcopalians have found this rite to be meaningful when they have experienced a significant renewal of their faith or when they have returned to active membership after having lapsed from the faith.

These changes were not merely imposed by a new Prayer Book. Rather, they reflect a gradual shift in the understanding and practice of Christian initiation. The twentieth century has been a time of liturgical renewal, not only in the Episcopal Church but also in other churches in the Anglican Communion and in other denominations, both Protestant and Catholic.

Associated Parishes, formed in 1946 to encourage revitalization of worship in the Episcopal Church, advocated public baptism during the main Sunday service and called for careful preparation of the parents and sponsors of infant candidates for baptism. Further impetus for public baptism came from the religious education movement which flourished in the Episcopal Church after the Second World War. As a result of this movement, many parishes instituted "family services" during the 1950s, and baptism increasingly came to be celebrated publicly during these services. By the time the 1979 Prayer Book was adopted, the rubric stating "Baptism is appropriately administered within the Eucharist as the chief service on a Sunday or other feast"[3] reflected what had already become the normative practice in many congregations.

As baptism gradually came to greater prominence in the life of the church, some clergy and laity began to question the confirmation rubric. Since baptism is the primary sacrament of Christian initiation and conversion, they argued, should not baptism rather than confirmation be the basis for admission to communion? Religious educators pointed to the ability of young children to appreciate and learn from sacramental actions, and suggested that children might best learn about communion by participating in it. Such discussions led in a few parishes and dioceses to experiments with "early" admission to communion before work had begun on Prayer Book revision.

The shift to public baptism, a new emphasis on the preparation of parents and sponsors, and the admission to communion of baptized but unconfirmed persons are indicative of a growing recognition of the centrality of baptism in Christian life. This baptismal renewal was accompanied by a new understanding of ministry. Instead of looking upon clergy as *the* ministers of the church, Episcopalians began to speak about "the ministry of the laity." As a result, the Catechism in the 1979 Prayer Book states, "The ministers of the Church are lay persons, bishops, priests, and deacons."[4]

Changing perceptions of ministry involved not only a new emphasis on lay ministry, but also a new awareness that baptism, not confirmation, is the basis for Christian ministry. It had become common to hear confirmation described as the lay person's ordination, the time when baptized persons were strengthened and sent forth as ministers in the world. But by the early 1960s, this view of confirmation was disputed. Massey Shepherd, lecturing at General Seminary in 1964, insisted that baptism rather than confirmation should be seen as the "ordination of the laity."[5] In a 1963 pamphlet issued by the Department of Christian Education of the Episcopal Church, Chauncie Kilmer Myers (who became Bishop of California in 1966) emphasized that all who are baptized into the Body of Christ are commissioned to participate in Christ's ministry of service to the world. The pamphlet concluded with a call to Christians to rediscover the meaning of baptism and thus rediscover the church's ministry to the world.[6]

This renewed understanding of baptism as foundational for Christian ministry is an important dimension of the rite of Holy Baptism in the 1979 Prayer Book. In the Baptismal Covenant those about to be baptized (or the parents and sponsors of infants and young children) join with those already baptized and promise to "proclaim by word and example the Good News of God in Christ," to "seek and serve Christ in all persons," to "strive for justice and peace among all people," and to "respect the dignity of every human being." The Prayers for the Candidates include a petition to "send them into the world in witness to [God's] love."[7] The catechumenate (a process preparing adults for baptism) includes an exploration of the catechumen's gifts for ministry and expects that catechumens will begin participating in a life of Christian service.[8]

The 1979 Prayer Book thus represents a growing understanding of baptism as the foundation for Christian life and ministry. But the new rites were preceded by over two decades of theological reflection and changing liturgical practices. So also is the Episcopal Church only gradually realizing the full implications of the 1979 Prayer Book, as A. Theodore Eastman, Bishop of Maryland, has suggested: "If used properly, taken seriously, and followed to its logical conclusions, the [1979] rite of Holy Baptism *could* revolutionize the liturgical, political, educational, and missionary life of the Episcopal Church."[9]

The essays in this book are offered as a contribution to the continuing theological discussion and efforts to renew liturgical practice. The authors address underlying issues and offer concrete suggestions for liturgical reform consonant with the 1979 Prayer Book.

In "Decoding the Obvious," William Seth Adams explores the extent to which our reawakening to the centrality of baptism has taken root in the liturgical life of the Episcopal Church. Examining both spatial evidence (the placement and use of the baptismal font) and ritual evidence (baptismal practice as compared to ordination practice), Adams offers a thought-provoking critique of our practice of both baptism and ordination, and the implications thereof for the ministry of all the baptized. The final section of his essay offers practical guidance for parishes wanting to evaluate and reform their baptismal practice so that they might achieve a fuller expression of the power and centrality of baptism in Christian life.

Adams also presents the possibility, without offering specific recommendations, that ordination rites might point to baptism as the foundation for ministry. While such proposals are beyond the scope of this volume, two essays address rites related to ordained ministry: the Celebration of a New Ministry (BCP 1979, pp. 557-65) and the Reaffirmation of Ordination Vows, found in *The Book of Occasional Services*.[10]

Stephen Kelsey's essay, "Celebrating Baptismal Ministry at the Welcoming of New Ministers," considers the issues involved when a congregation welcomes a new leader. As Kelsey points out, even the term "new minister" is problematic because all baptized newcomers to a parish are ministers. But the issues go beyond terminology. How can a congregation formally celebrate its new relationship with a leader, typically a cleric, in a manner which also affirms the continuing ministry of the congregation and its members? Kelsey emphasizes the mutuality between (ordained) church leaders and all the baptized, a mutuality in which both cleric and congregants find their baptismal ministries developed by Christ, a mutuality in which the congregation participates in the development of the new minister's leadership.

Kelsey concludes by reviewing the Celebration of a New Ministry and offering alternatives which serve to emphasize the ministry of all the baptized. The 1979 Prayer Book service, a significant revision of the earlier Prayer Book office for the institution of new ministers, offers considerable latitude. Many of the rubrics read "may" rather than "shall," and in several places the rubrics suggest that a text other than the one provided may be used.[11] This flexibility has led to experimentation in several parishes and dioceses, often in an effort to affirm the ministry of all the baptized. Kelsey's suggestions are designed to help a planning group comprising congregational leaders, including the new minister, design a celebration that expresses the role of the new minister in the context of the baptismal ministries of the congregation and the mutual relationship being established.

The relationship of ordination to baptism is also addressed by Michael Hopkins in his essay, "The Reaffirmation of Ordination Vows." Noting that this rite is used in many dioceses on Maundy Thursday or during Holy Week in conjunction with the Consecration of Chrism, Hopkins challenges the juxtaposition of these two rites. He goes on to question a Reaffirmation of Ordination Vows which is principally a clergy event with few, if any, laity present and which has no clear relation to baptism. Instead, Hopkins maintains, the primary recommitment to ministry for both clergy and laity occurs in every celebration of Eucharist. Every Eucharist is a renewal of our baptismal union with Christ and thus is a renewal of our commitment to participate in Christ's ministry of reconciliation in the world. Hopkins concludes by suggesting alternatives to the current Reaffirmation of Ordination Vows and a different setting for the Consecration of Chrism Apart from Baptism.[12]

The careful reader may note some discrepancy between, on the one hand, Kelsey's proposals for a Celebration of a New Ministry that emphasizes the ministry of all the baptized and, on the other hand, Hopkins' proposal that the Celebration of a New Ministry include the reaffirmation of ordination vows (although Hopkins notes that this must be set within the context of the ministry of all the baptized). As the church comes to a renewed understanding of baptismal ministry, it may be appropriate to experiment with several different proposals in order to develop ordination rites and related rites that speak powerfully about the ministry of all baptized persons.

In the concluding essay of this collection our attention is turned toward the Episcopal Church's understanding and practice of Confirmation and Reception. The 1979 rite of Confirmation includes a formula for receiving baptized persons affiliating with the Episcopal Church but does not specify the distinction between confirmation and reception. The result has been a wide diversity of policy and practice, and no little confusion. In "To Confirm or To Receive?" Daniel Stevick explores the historical, pastoral, ecumenical, and theological dimensions of this question. Emphasizing the significance of Baptism as the sacrament of complete Christian initiation, he recommends that the Episcopal Church receive rather than confirm those who have been baptized and come to mature faith in other Christian traditions.

In his discussion of confirmation and reception, Stevick refers to and builds upon an essay by Charles Price, "Rites of Initiation," first issued in September 1984 as an Occasional Paper of the Standing Liturgical Commission. Because Price provides useful historical and theological background, with particular attention to the development of the rites in the 1979 Prayer Book, his essay is included as an Appendix to this volume.

Both Price and Stevick emphasize that baptized persons become members of the Episcopal Church by having their baptisms duly recorded in this church.[13] Yet other portions of the Constitution and Canons of the Episcopal Church require that persons be baptized and confirmed in order to minister within the church, for example, as a Lay Eucharistic Minister or a Deputy to General Convention. This requirement for confirmation appears to undermine the Prayer Book statement that Holy Baptism is *full* Christian initiation and to go beyond the assertion that confirmation is *expected* (not required) of all adult members of the Episcopal Church.[14] As the Episcopal Church comes to understand the implications of the theological premise that baptism is the basis for all Christian ministry, it may be appropriate to reconsider these canonical requirements for ministry within the church. Perhaps a more appropriate standard would be that of "adult communicant in good standing," which the Canons define as a member (baptized person whose baptism is duly recorded), sixteen years of age or over, who has received communion at least three times during the preceding year and has been faithful in corporate worship and in working, praying, and giving for the spread of the Kingdom of God.[15]

Canonical requirements for those who minister within the Episcopal Church are but one implication of the 1979 Prayer Book rites of Holy Baptism and Confirmation, with forms for Reception and for the Reaffirmation of Baptismal Vows. These essays are offered in the hope that the Episcopal Church will come to a fuller realization of the many implications of understanding baptism as the basis for the Christian life of ministry both within the church and in the world.

I extend my appreciation to the authors of these essays for their contributions to this collection and their willingness to respond to the requests of the Standing Liturgical Commission. William Seth Adams' essay, "Decoding the Obvious," appeared in an earlier form in *Worship*, Vol. 66 (July 1992), pp. 327-38, and is reprinted here with permission. "Rites of Initiation," by Charles P. Price, appeared in *The Occasional Papers of the Standing Liturgical Commission*, Collection Number One (Church Hymnal, 1987), pp. 24-37.

The Reverend Ruth A. Meyers
All Saints' Day, 1993

NOTES

1. The Book of Common Prayer 1979, p. 298. (Hereinafter referred to as BCP 1979.)

2. Ibid., p. 312.

3. Ibid., p. 298.

4. Ibid., p. 855.

5. *Liturgy and Education* (New York: Seabury, 1965), p. 106.

6. *Baptized into the One Church* (New York: Seabury, 1963).

7. BCP 1979, pp. 305-306.

8. *The Book of Occasional Services* 1991 (New York: Church Hymnal, 1991), pp. 112-113.

9. *The Baptizing Community* (New York: Seabury, 1982; revised edition, Morehouse, 1991), p. 4; emphasis added.

10. *BOS* 1991, pp. 231-234.

11. BCP 1979, pp. 559-565.

12. See *BOS* 1991, pp. 228-30, for the rite of Consecration of Chrism Apart from Baptism.

13. Canon I.17.1(a). See below: Stevick, p. 76, and Price, p. 95.

14. BCP 1979, pp. 298, 412; Canon I.17.1(c).

15. Canon I.17, Sections 1-3.

Decoding the Obvious: Reflections on Baptismal Ministry in the Episcopal Church

The Reverend William Seth Adams

I. Stating the Problem

The Episcopal Church is reawakening to the importance of Christian initiation.[1] The texts in The Book of Common Prayer and *The Book of Occasional Services* are the best signs and continuing sources of this reawakening. Clearly, the rites for baptism and the series of rites associated with the catechumenate, combined with the Prayer Book's directive regarding the public nature of initiation, the naming of baptismal days and the heightened place given the Easter Vigil in our ritual life all work to enhance and invigorate the church's baptismal practice.

In addition to these texts and rubrical norms, there are meetings, conferences and books which augment and interpret the liturgical texts, teaching and encouraging the church in its initiation practices. Among these are Daniel Stevick's *Baptismal Moments; Baptismal Meanings* (1987), *The Baptismal Mystery and the Catechumenate*, edited by Michael Merriman (1989), and the 1991 revised edition of A. Theodore Eastman's *The Baptizing Community* (1982). Further, in groups like the Associated Parishes and the Association of Diocesan Liturgy and Music Commissions, the Episcopal Church has people of deep concern and insight offering their gifts in pointed and programmatic forms to any and all interested.

From these and many other quarters, both within and without the Episcopal Church, efforts mount to empower the rites which make Christians, to give a true place to the complex ritual act which bestows forgiveness of sins and raises to newness of life, which seals by the Spirit of God and makes one Christ's own forever. In the face of all this, one must first of all cheer about this turn of events, and having cheered, as surely I do, then work to assist the enterprise.

It appears that the assistance I can offer is of a peculiar sort. That is, what I find myself able to do is to identify impediments to the process. In fact, I find myself convinced that the real and effectual power of Christian initiation in the Episcopal Church faces dismal prospects for true and faithful "success." This is so on two grounds, namely, spatial evidence and ritual evidence. What I intend to do in the following remarks is to examine this physical evidence with an eye to "decoding the obvious."[2]

In a way, what I am suggesting is that what we *claim* about the importance of initiation is not supported by the physical, observable evidence. This failure to support discredits our claims. And if evangelism is to be central to the work we are about, then surely this rite of conversion and incorporation needs to be healthy and to tell the truth to those drawn into the fellowship of Christ.

II. Spatial Evidence

The central ritual metaphor underneath all the rites in the Prayer Book is an encounter, an encounter between the gathered community and God. This encounter is acted out and experienced in the church's public liturgy around three liturgical centers within a common liturgical space. The three centers are the place for Baptism, the place for the Liturgy of the Word, and the place for the Liturgy at the Altar/Table.

The ecclesiology of the Prayer Book sees the church as a community.[3] Liturgically speaking, the work of this community is distributed among the several members and enacted in the gathering.

The clear supposition is that the community will all gather in the same room, rather than in several rooms, as in older architectural styles. (At its most extravagant, a Gothic building had three rooms—one for the baptized, one for the choir [clergy] and one for the ordained presider.)

In addition, because the liturgical work is distributed in a functional rather than hierarchical fashion, there is no need for the space to be hierarchically ordered, though clearly one must be sensitive to the needs of hearing and seeing. This way of viewing the space requires that we abandon the older names (nave, chancel, sanctuary) and search for new ones. Interestingly enough, so far as I can tell, the search has yet to yield a really usable vocabulary.

In addition to a single room, this view of the church requires a configuration that in a tangible way sets forth testimony to "gathering around." This leads to the abandonment of the linear, rectangular building (the one modeled on the bus) in favor of some configuration several-sided around the central focus. This notion tends to create a room that is wider than it is deep. A circular configuration has attracted some, though under most circumstances I would argue against the circle on both practical and theological grounds.[4]

If a single chamber is most congruent with the intent of the Prayer Book, the interrelationship of the liturgical centers within that space is our next concern. In Marion Hatchett's Occasional Paper, "Architectural Implications of The Book of Common Prayer," he says that the three liturgical centers—the place for Baptism, the place for Liturgy of the Word and the place for the Liturgy at the Altar/Table—"should have approximately equal dignity and prominence."[5]

My own way of expressing this is to view the liturgical space as if it were an ecosystem, an interactive community of organisms within an environment. This way of understanding the existence and organization of space puts the *interrelationship* of these centers on equal footing with their own particular and individual integrity.

A sound ecosystem is dependent on mutual necessity and reciprocity. Consequently, as a metaphor for the character of a liturgical space, an ecosystem establishes *balance* as a central characteristic.

The ambo and altar/table constitute two of the three liturgical centers which populate our liturgical environment. The baptismal space is the third, and the principal concern of this essay.

Surely there is no subject in liturgical studies more warmly or richly treated in our time than baptismal rites and theology. Human concern for identity, membership and initiation coupled with ever greater curiosity about the activity of God's Holy Spirit have brought out of us more and more powerful convictions about this rite of burial, birth and bathing.

"Holy Baptism is full initiation by water and the Holy Spirit into Christ's Body the Church. The bond which God establishes in Baptism is indissoluble."[6] So reads the Prayer Book. Although debates still arise throughout the church as to what confirmation is, the importance and centrality of the water rite are not in dispute. Consequently, and in principle at least, there is also no debate about the importance of the ritual object which must bear the symbolic weight of our initiation theology. The rubrics imagine a place, a container, a pool of such size as to make possible the immersion of an adult.

Efforts in evidence in the Prayer Book to restore baptism to its rightful place and to give substance and symbolic power to the ritual object necessary for baptism have been fostered in large measure by a deeply held conviction about the calling of the baptized and the theological centrality of baptism. Theodore Eastman has spoken for many in saying, "baptism is ordination to the principal order of ministry."[7] In an important book, *Anglicanism and the Christian Church*, Paul Avis calls baptism "the fundamental sacrament of Christianity" and "the ground of our unity." Further, he proposes a *"baptismal paradigm"* as the starting point for the church's own self-understanding and for conversations with other Christians.[8] Put another way, this suggests that the faith of "the blessed company of all faithful people" should be our primary place to stand rather than to require exclusively the company of "the successors of the apostles." This would provide us an ecclesiology formed on baptism, not ordination.

The foregoing suggests that at one level the Episcopal Church's teaching about baptism works to give the rite power, centrality, and authenticity. In practice, however, and in powerfully subtle ways, the current state of the physical evidence among us puts the lie to what we say.

In the spring and summer of 1990, with the aid of the Episcopal Church's Board for Theological Education, the Conant Fund and the Episcopal Theological Seminary of the Southwest, I completed a six-month sabbatical leave. The time was spent exploring the state of contemporary liturgical architecture in the Episcopal Church. To put it minimally, I was looking to see what we are building for ourselves, and in some way assessing the current work against the architectural and liturgical assumptions of the Prayer Book.

I made formal visits to thirty-one congregations across the United States.[9] Of the total, nineteen buildings had been built or reordered since 1980. In each visit I observed and photographed the liturgical space and made a drawing of the floor plan. In addition, by means of questionnaires designed for the purpose, I gathered information from the rector/vicar, musicians, members of the congregation and the architect/designer as to how the space "works."

With specific regard to the place for baptism (and based on this sample of thirty-one places), line drawings would suggest that typically fonts were placed near entrances, on a main aisle, in their own niche or in the "east" end near the altar/table and ambo. These characteristics, alone or in combination, suggest that these fonts were in "correct" places. At the same time, of the places visited, four had no font in evidence. Of these four, two had small tables available on which bowls were placed when needed.

Only one of the sites visited would suggest to the observer that this room for proclamation and table fellowship is also a room for baptism. The ritual object in this particular liturgical space would (almost) bear the theological weight our teaching would place upon it and would (almost) allow to happen what the rubrics presuppose. In virtually no other instance, perhaps with one exception, did the Prayer Book's renewed emphasis on baptism stimulate a more powerful spatial expression of our baptismal theology. Typically, I found small stone or wooden fonts, sometimes covered, sometimes not, sometimes containing a "candy dish," sometimes not, typically empty of water. Occasionally, it was clear to the observer that the most frequent role played by the font, particularly those near entrances, was as a place to set things, e.g., service leaflets.

During this tour across the country and the church, I was reminded again and again how powerful a symbol the altar/table is (often protected by rails, elevated spatially, adorned with special "clothing," typically approached and touched only by certain people, characterized by physical stability and permanence) and how subject to disregard the font is (hidden away or absent, minimal in size, empty, trivialized in use). I was reminded again and again that ordained people attend the altar/table and that the (typically) incidental font is allegedly the place of empowerment of the baptized. I was thereby taught that the theological claims made for baptism were seriously challenged, even undermined, by the subtle and persistent disjuncture between our claims and the physical evidence.

III. Ritual Evidence

If the spatial evidence signals an impediment to the success of our theological claims about the importance of baptism and the centrality to the Episcopal Church of the ministry of the baptized, the second stumbling block, in my view, is the difficulty created for our baptismal theology by a comparison of the baptismal rite and ordination. It is my opinion that claims about the empowerment for ministry associated with baptism will likely never find full expression so long as the rite of baptism is overshadowed by the rite of ordination. And ordination language in association with baptism will, frankly, only make things worse.

In order to make this point more clear, a "tour" of these two rites, baptism and ordination, seems appropriate. (Given my life's work in a seminary, I probably attend more ordinations than most people, certainly more than the typical parishioner, and likely more than is good for me. At the same time, the experience does give me a particularly good place from which to observe.) The following descriptions will necessarily lead to comparison.

Both of these are rites of passage, rites which are typically composed of three particular parts. The first part accomplishes the *separation* of the person(s) from their former status in the community; the second part accomplishes the *transition*, the passage intended; and the third part accomplishes the *reintegration* of the person(s) into the community. The transition phase is when "something happens," as it were. It is the most dynamic in ritual terms, the densest in meaning and, consequently, the most significant for our consideration. We shall therefore examine in turn the transition phase of the rites for baptism and presbyteral ordination as contained in The Book of Common Prayer.

In the baptismal liturgy, the transition phase begins with the movement of the baptismal party to the font if they are not there already. Here the water is poured if it has not already been poured and the water is blessed. The prayer formula begins in a way reminiscent of the Great Thanksgiving in the Eucharist. "The Lord be with you./And also with you." "Let us give thanks to the Lord our God./It is right to give him thanks and praise." Following a reiteration of the role water plays in salvation history, the one who presides invokes the activity of God's Holy Spirit to sanctify the water. The rite assumes at this point that there is more than one candidate so the rubrics direct that each receive the water in turn. The "watering" then follows. After all have received the action of the water, the presider "in full sight of the congregation" prays for the sustaining power of the Holy Spirit and signs the forehead of each with a cross (and perhaps oil). Supplementary rubrics say the newly baptized may be given a candle. This is obviously not central. They are then welcomed by the assembly and thus reintegrated into the community. The peace of the Lord is exchanged, and the newly baptized return to their seats in the assembly. The fact that the newly baptized have completed their transition (the passage) is fully expressed later in the rite by their admission to the fellowship of the altar/table.

We should notice that this rite is appropriately administered within the Sunday Eucharist and especially appropriate on five occasions mentioned in the supplementary rubrics at the end of the rite.[10] Although the bishop is (historically) the normative presider, in practice it is typically a presbyter who presides.

Turning now to the rite for the ordination of a presbyter, we engage it at the comparable ritual moment, the moment of transition. All present are directed to stand, except the candidate who must kneel before the bishop, the necessary presider. The candidate is joined left and right by other presbyters. The clear supposition here is that there is just one candidate. (The supplemental rubrics printed at the end of the ordinal allow the possibility of more than one but this is obviously exceptional.) A hymn calling upon the Spirit is sung followed by a prescribed silence. The bishop offers a prayer of thanks after which he or she places both hands on the head of the candidate. The presbyters also lay on hands. The bishop then prays that God will fill the candidate with grace and power through the gift of the Spirit. Removing all the hands, the bishop continues in prayer petitioning God on behalf of the newly ordained. Following this prayer, the people are directed to respond "Amen" in a loud voice. The newly ordained is given appropriate vesture and the Bible, this latter as a sign of authority. The transition now accomplished, the process of reintegration is begun by the bishop greeting the newly ordained, who in turn extends the peace of the Lord to the assembly. The attending presbyters are directed by rubric to greet the newly ordained.

I hope I have described these rites so that their content and movement are clear. In each case, what I have described is part of a larger ritual event and each transitional phase is followed by the liturgy of Holy Communion. The differences between these rites are remarkable.

Presbyteral ordinations are typically understood to be preceded by an extended period of preparation (seminary), parochial sponsorship, testing and assessment (Commissions on Ministry and the General Ordination Exams) and an apprenticeship (diaconate). Baptisms are typically not.

Ordinations take place in public at special times, with attendance by invitation. Baptisms take place in public but typically within the conventional Sunday liturgy. Invitations are not customary. Ordinations are usually attended by clergy who are vested, enter in procession and sit in a prominent place in the assembly. This is not typical of baptisms. Ordinations are rites reserved to bishops, the chief liturgical officer. Baptisms may be, but in practice usually are not. The rite of presbyteral ordination assumes only one candidate. Baptism presupposes more than one candidate. Ordinations are frequently filled with special music and festive ornaments. This is less so with baptisms.

The entrance rite for an ordination is built around the person of the ordinand, who has entered the room in procession accompanied by sponsors. The entrance rite for baptism is special to the occasion but is not built around the candidates, who typically have entered with the congregation and have not been a part of the entrance procession.

The readings for ordinations are specifically chosen for the rite and occasion, whereas the typical readings for baptism are the proper readings assigned to the Sunday liturgy. The preacher at an ordination is usually invited with great care and feeling by the ordinand. This is usually not the case at baptisms. In ordination sermons, there is typically a charge directed toward the ordinand. This is not so common at baptisms.

Ordinations take place at the "east" end of the liturgical space, the "front" so to say, toward which all the seats face and where the lighting and acoustics are generally good. In the "conventional"

Episcopal Church, baptisms occur in the back of the room, at the west end, behind the assembly, "off-center," where lighting is often not sufficient and acoustics are often poor.

In the ordination rite, the moment of transition is accomplished with great force, signaled by the heading atop the page, "The Consecration of the Priest."[11] After the hymn invoking the Spirit a corporate silence is kept. Following a necessary silence, the candidate is surrounded or "buried" as it were in a heavy layer of hands, presbyteral as well as episcopal hands. Hands are the agents here of the sacrament. In contrast, at the transitional moment in conventional baptismal practice, titled "The Baptism," a minimal amount of sacramental "stuff" is used (that is, a few drops of water) and it is typically dried off almost immediately lest anyone get wet!

Finally, whereas the newly baptized return to their seats in the assembly, where they were seated before, the newly ordained is invited "to take a higher seat," in proximity to the altar/table. In this way, the change of status is demonstrated.

Where does this comparison lead? To what conclusion do we come?

In the narrow view, it seems that the ritual power of the ordination rite exceeds in practice that of baptism. At no step in our comparison does the action of baptism (as conventionally practiced) speak more loudly than ordination at a comparable point. Indeed, the ritual patterns upon which ordinations are built appear to be a combination of the wedding rite and coronation. Baptism, on the other hand, has only its own self as its pattern, it being already a rite of incorporation. Certainly, the "spectacle" of the two is quite different.

It may seem harsh to say it, but on the basis of this comparison, what we want to claim about baptism and "the principal order of ministry" is ritual nonsense. And so long as that remains true, our teaching, however wise and faithful, however substantive and compelling, will be defeated by our ritual actions, which by this test contradict our theology.

IV. Conclusions

In its simplest terms, I have suggested and (I believe) demonstrated that, in the Episcopal Church context, the truth told by our baptismal rite and the teachings we offer about it are not supported by our spatial and ritual evidence. Until such time as they are, we ought not to anticipate real empowerment for ministry of the baptized. (In addition, we ought to anticipate the criticism from some quarter that "we" [clergy, perhaps] are really perfectly happy about that.) In the face of this evidence, it is surely a sign of God's benevolence to the church that the ministry of the baptized is as powerful as it is.

Behind this conclusion lies a particular theoretical perspective which has provided the methodology for this exploration. This perspective has two dimensions—ritual congruence and ritual coherence.

"Ritual congruence" signals the integrity, health, and veracity of any particular ritual event; its absence signals the opposite. We come to congruence by analyzing the relationship of four aspects of any liturgical event. Firstly, there are obviously the *texts* themselves, the scripts, so to say. Insofar as The Book of Common Prayer is concerned, this would include not only the ritual text but also the rubrical material. Secondly, there is the *ritual action*, the work of the ritual community, which accompanies, animates and accomplishes the texts. Thirdly, there is the *environment* within which the action takes place, the setting, the things used. Lastly, all these exist and operate within a kind of *interpretive framework*, a theological understanding, a hermeneutic, as it were, which is admittedly and necessarily historically conditioned and contextual. In its healthier moments, the history of the church's liturgical tradition is marked by a high degree of ritual congruence among these four. In times of ill health, the absence of congruence has typically and eventually led to reform.

"Ritual congruence" then is a term aimed at the internal integrity of a rite, the ability of a ritual event "to tell the truth." I have suggested above that by this test, the baptismal liturgy of the Episcopal Church is not "congruent."

In addition to internal congruence, however, there is yet another point of assessment, namely, the correlation between a given rite and other rites in the complex. This second point of assessment is "ritual coherence." Beyond the initial question of the internal integrity of a rite, one must also examine the comparative claims made by various rites and, on this second basis as well, render judgment. An analogy here might be found in ecumenical conversation. What Anglicans say in dialogue with Lutherans, for example, must have its own internal sense ("congruence"), and it must also make sense when put alongside what we say to Roman Catholics and the Orthodox ("coherence"). I have suggested above that when the rites of baptism and presbyteral ordination are compared with each other, ritual coherence is not achieved.

I am persuaded, along with many others, that the ritual life of a community is formative of that community. For us, that means that the liturgy is formative of the church. In the liturgy, in the midst of our praise of God, we remember and act out our identity. We describe to ourselves who we are, what we intend and hope for. It is on this basis that the absence of congruence and coherence regarding the baptismal liturgy has its subtle and unremitting impact on the self-understanding of the Episcopal Church.

Access to resolution of this problem is easier in spatial terms than in ritual terms. Such spaces would be proximate to the assembly, near a major entry, either visually accessible from congregational seating or located in an open area large enough for many of the congregation to gather about the font. The font itself would be of considerable size, preferably a pool in the ground, though a raised font might also serve. In each case, water would be present, ideally flowing ("living") water. The location of the font and the presence of the water would invite those who enter to encounter again the water of baptism, and if given to such things, to make again the sign of the cross.[12]

Resolving the ritual problem is more difficult, since the conventional methods of liturgical reform and revision are rooted in the gradual evolution of rites, tested primarily by historical norms. What appears to me to be necessary is something quite different. First, we need to take seriously Paul Avis's tantalizing suggestion, mentioned earlier, that we fix our ecclesiology to a "baptismal paradigm." Commitment to such a paradigm would force us to talk more clearly about ministry in baptismal terms (as we struggle to do now) and then require us to ask the following ritual question: What would an ordination rite look/feel like that saw itself as dependent upon and derivative from the baptismal rite? In other words, what would an ordination rite look like that, as a by-product of its main intention, taught that the principal order of ministry in the church was brought into being elsewhere? What a revolutionary notion! It might be very interesting to see.[13]

V. Epilogue

The coherence question, inclusive as it is of multiple rites, must remain to another time to explore beyond the tantalizing suggestion made above. The matter of congruence, however, needs our attention, since the pursuit of this question could have direct consequences on the life and spirit of congregations, even without the further revision of texts.

If a congregation were to address itself to the question of congruence in its baptismal practice, given the rite(s) we now possess, how might this be done? Assuming certain conventions, common to Episcopal church buildings of a typical sort, there are certain considerations, which, if explored, would bring into greater alignment what we do and what we say.

At the outset, we should remember that "congruence" is to be understood as the happy relationship of four ingredients: texts (including rubrical material), ritual action, environment and the interpretive framework in which they reside. Since the liturgy itself is our great teacher and its cumulative power is formative of the church, a congregation seeking congruence is best advised to make careful assessment of its own lived-out experience on these four points. Deliberate truth seeking of this sort will lead to suggestions for greater congruence. (This kind of review might most profitably be done by an educated parish liturgy committee.)

For education in the pursuit of this assessment, the primary source is obviously the Prayer Book itself, but Theodore Eastman's book *The Baptizing Community* is a very useful companion. Reading the Prayer Book rites is the necessary first step.

What naturally follows, then, is a set of questions and concerns which could inform such an assessment. Consideration of these kinds of questions will help to clarify the parish's current practice and to give direction for change as needed.

First, as to textual considerations, this would necessarily involve a thorough review of the initiation rites in the Prayer Book, seeking to explore what the rites intend to provide. Careful attention would need to be given both to the rubrical directions and particularly to the theological content of the rite. In assessing the textual materials, it is likely that some measure of new awareness will begin to develop in those charged with the assessment. Study of the texts themselves often proves illuminating. For example, the careful reader will discover that whereas in the experience of most congregations, the normal (meaning the most commonly observed) baptismal candidate is an infant, the rite itself clearly assumes someone able to speak for themselves (an adult?) as the *normative* candidate, that is, the candidate the rite "has in mind." This same careful reader will also discover a richness of theological language and images still not clearly visible in the lived-out experience of baptized communities.

Secondly, consideration would need to be given to the ritual practice of the parish. How is the action of baptism accomplished? Are the baptismal days, as encouraged in the Prayer Book, followed in the parish? Are "private" baptisms done and under what circumstances? What value does water have in the parish's ritual bathing? (This seems a foolish question but the answer can be quite illuminating, given that water is the operative symbol in the rite.) How does the baptismal party enter the celebration (remembering that at ordinations, for example, the recipient of the sacramental action is a participant in the entrance procession, along with presenters/sponsors)? Do the sponsors do what the liturgy invites? On the baptismal days, in congregations in which multiple Sunday services are the norm, are baptisms celebrated at each or no? Or is there one central celebration at which the "whole" congregation is present? All these questions intend to invite an exploration of what actually goes on in the congregation's current practice of Christian initiation.

Thirdly, the liturgical environment for baptism would need analysis. Since most Episcopal churches do not have fonts that would allow immersion, even of infants, the question arises as to how to make a modest pedestal font as fitting a symbol as possible of the remarkable power of baptismal washing. Is the font a constant presence in the liturgical space or does it "appear" on certain festivals? Where is it placed, by an entry or somewhere else? Is it placed so that people "encounter" it during the course of the liturgy, or even on a non-liturgical visit to the space? Is the font approachable and welcoming, or separated and enclosed, perhaps with rails and suchlike? If the font has a cover, is it typically left on or left off the font? Is water kept continuously in the font, such that parishioners and any visitor might have the opportunity to engage the water on entering and leaving the space? (Many people, given the opportunity, will take the water upon their hand and make the sign of the cross, a regular and tactile remembrance of one's own baptism.)

Another issue related to the liturgical environment is the nature of the lighting associated with the font. Are the font and the baptismal area lighted sufficiently, and does the degree of illumination testify to the mutuality of altar, ambo and font? Further, what is the nature of the vesture and other ornaments associated with the parish's baptismal practice? Is sufficient dignity accorded to the baptismal rite by this means? (In considering this particular question, one ought to remember that the font itself and the water it contains are powerful and primary symbols. The use of symbols upon symbols, therefore, must be evaluated with great care. Simple eloquent elements speak their own power.)

Finally, as to the environment, care needs to be taken as to how the font and its associated area are treated when not in ritual use. Put bluntly, is the edge of the font used as a place where things (leaflets, etc.) are "stored" as if on an end table? Is the area surrounding the font treated with proper dignity or is it frequently filled with folding chairs, for example, awaiting later use? (Though surely the common possession of the church, the font should not be treated as if a "common" object.)

Turning now to the fourth element in achieving congruence— the interpretive framework—several issues warrant attention. Perhaps the most important matter to explore is the nature of preaching and teaching in the parish about baptism and its place in the life of the church. What is the proclamation on baptismal days? Beyond this issue, what is the character, content and duration of catechesis in the parish for those preparing for baptism and/or sponsorship? Is the sponsorship of baptismal candidates an identifiable ministry in the parish? Does catechesis continue after baptism? Are the claims made in the parish about the nature of baptism and the ministry of the baptized acted out by clergy and laity alike? Does the parish understand itself as a "baptizing community"?

Another matter, smaller in proportion but telling nonetheless, is the question of the preparation of the parish congregation itself for baptismal occasions. Each time the church baptizes, the church experiences a change in itself. Is the congregation, in preparation for this baptismal change, given occasion to prepare itself to receive new members? Is notice given in advance of the baptismal days, declaring that on a day forthcoming, the congregation will witness death and resurrection, rebirth and initiation?

This set of issues and questions constitutes only suggestions as to how a particular parish might pursue congruence in its own practice of Christian initiation. My hope is that the results of such exploration might issue in a liturgical congruence that would give bold testimony to the place of baptism in the life of the Episcopal Church. Whether by this means or some other, there is surely ample reason to ponder the reality of our parochial (or diocesan) initiatory practice, with an eye to its enrichment. This is, after all, the Decade of Evangelism, a time dedicated to the making of new Christians and the upbuilding of the life of the church, a time begging for a remembered and lived-out liturgical theology which truthfully "decodes the obvious," thereby acknowledging this rite of burial, birth and bath as the centerpiece and organizing principle of ministry for all faithful people.[14]

NOTES

1. Some of these ideas formed a part of one of the Rossiter Lectures I delivered at Bexley Hall, Rochester, N.Y., in the fall of 1988. I express my thanks to the Dean and Board for that invitation.

2. I am borrowing here the language of my friend and colleague, Charles James Cook.

3. See BCP 1979, p. 854.

4. For those interested in this, see my article "An Apology for Variable Liturgical Space," *Worship* 61 (1987): pp. 240-241.

5. *The Occasional Papers of the Standing Liturgical Commission,* Collection Number One (New York: Church Hymnal, 1987), p. 58.

6. BCP 1979, p. 298.

7. *The Baptizing Community* (Harrisburg, PA: Morehouse, revised edition, 1991), p. 35.

8. *Anglicanisn and the Christian Church* (Minneapolis: Fortress, 1989), pp. 303-304.

9. Sites were visited in California, Illinois, Minnesota, Washington, Texas, Oregon, Missouri, Virginia and the District of Columbia.

10. These are the Easter Vigil, the Day of Pentecost, All Saints' Day or the Sunday following, the Feast of the Baptism of Jesus (the first Sunday after the Epiphany) and the occasion of the Bishop's visitation. BCP 1979, p. 312.

11. BCP 1979, p. 533.

12. I have seen good examples of the sort of space I describe here in several Roman Catholic churches, for example, St. John the Evangelist, Hopkins, Minnesota; the Chapel of the Incarnation at the University of Dallas, Dallas, Texas; and the Church of St. Francis of Assisi, Concord, California. Among Episcopal churches that I know, I would cite the baptismal area in Grace Cathedral, San Francisco, and St. Matthew's Church, Pacific Palisades, California.

13. I know of efforts in this direction in the Episcopal Diocese of Northern Michigan in which Bishop Thomas Ray has sought to associate baptism and ordination in the same ritual event. The texts used are those from The Book of Common Prayer.

14. Many insights in this final section were contributed by my friend and former student, Amy Donohue.

Celebrating Baptismal Ministry at the Welcoming of New Ministers*

The Reverend Stephen M. Kelsey

The welcoming of new leaders is an exciting moment in the life of a congregation. Many have high hopes for the new beginning. Old feuds and disappointments are put aside as members reaffirm their commitment to the source of their common life and mission. Often the arrival of a new leader has been preceded by a time of self-examination and planning by the congregation, which can bring considerable healing and reconciliation. Relationships are restored with neighboring congregations, and new leadership often emerges. Many discover a renewed sense of self-esteem as they celebrate what they have accomplished together while others labeled them "vacant."[1] It can also be a time when the people of a congregation remember who they are called to be, not just in relation to one, prominent, usually clerical personality, but as a community of the baptized in their own right: *"a ministering community, rather than a community gathered around a minister,"* as Bishop Wesley Frensdorff liked to say.[2]

But for others, it is a traumatic time. Some encounter unresolved personal issues as they grieve the loss of things as they have

---

*NOTE: I am not particularly comfortable with the term "new minister" as used in this context. Any person new to a congregation might rightly be referred to in this way, in that all share in ministry. Yet, to be consistent with the existing rite of our Prayer Book, "Celebration of a New Ministry," I will use the term "new minister" throughout this essay to refer to a person newly arrived in a congregation who will be taking a formal leadership role, whether that person be ordained or not.

been. Does affirmation of new leaders involve rejection of those to whom we were committed before? Leaders, ordained or not, continuing in the congregation may be uncertain as to whether in this new chapter in the life of this congregation their contribution will continue to be welcome. Similarly, the new minister, while excited about the new start, may be uncertain as to how his or her relationship with the members of this new congregation will emerge. "Who could live up to all these hopes and expectations?"

At this crucial moment, the congregation gathers with the bishop and representatives of other congregations and community organizations for a "Celebration of a New Ministry" to mark the beginning of a new chapter in their life together. In the context of this swirl of anxious energy and emotions, all attention, typically, is focused upon the new minister. Even the title of the liturgy encourages this: "celebrating the new ministry" (i.e., the new "cure") of the new minister him or herself, rather than the continuing life of that ministering Christian community. Is the local congregation considered significant primarily as an arena in which professional clergy ply their trade? The liturgy is planned and observed with a passion often reserved for marriages or coronations. In the background, one can almost hear variations on the theme from "*Mighty Mouse*"—"*Here he comes, to save the day!*"—so intent is everyone on convincing themselves and one another that they have found the one and only person appropriate to lead this congregation into a new day!

The rite for the "Celebration of a New Ministry" can easily take such a turn. Engraved invitations are sent out, honoring both the new minister and the congregation on their marvelous good fortune in finding one another. The analogy to marriage is not lost, with many thus assuming that the relationship is meant to last until death, retirement,...or until something goes wrong. And so the dissolution of any pastoral relationship tends to carry with it a suspicion of blame or shame...for someone. I can remember being welcomed into a new congregation as Rector while simultaneously another family arrived. There was no fanfare or special liturgy for them, although they were at least as serious about their faith as was I, and were to contribute equally to the life and mission of the congregation over the next few years. But it seemed so important to everyone that the arrival of the new cleric be marked with grandeur. I left the ceremony with a clear understanding that, by virtue of my ordination and institutional status, my ministry was considered crucial to the life of the congregation, while that of others was merely supportive or incidental.

This practice is not intentionally mean–spirited toward anyone. The anxiety of forming new relationships in the congregation can encourage an escalated effort to make the new minister and his or her family feel welcome. But it raises a question as to whether our practice in inducting new leaders perpetuates the notion that ministry is primarily the province of the ordained, with the others being either recipients or, if they are extraordinary, supporters of the ministry of the ordained. Can we, in the excitement of the arrival of a new leader, reaffirm the ministry of all the baptized as the foundation of the life of the congregation? How are we, in this liturgy, to make it clear that this new minister has arrived not to *replace*, but to *support* the continuing ministry and leadership of all the baptized in this congregation?

As we grow in our understanding of baptism, rather than ordination, as the primary sacrament of ministry, we will want to reconsider the shape that this liturgy takes. So many cultural forces around us impose expectations and advice as to how "the minister" should behave and be treated. In Christ, we are called to reach beyond those expectations to pattern a life in which no one member or segment of the community, no matter what their status within the church or in the world at large, dominates our attention or activity; in which the gifts and contributions of *all* the baptized are known to be equally precious, equally necessary to the life and mission of the church. What would it look like if all members of the community of faith were successful at bringing out the best in one another, engaging and supporting all people in ministry, both within the church gathered and in the church dispersed, in their daily lives? This we seek to rehearse, to "practice" now in our liturgy.[3]

Why Do We Need a Liturgy for Welcoming New Ministers?

Consider an occasion of the "welcoming of a new minister" in a congregation when this liturgy would *not* be necessary: the ordination of a "local priest" or "local deacon" (using "Canon 9"). In this case, the "new minister" is a member of long standing of that community, called by that community to serve among them. There is a natural integrity to such an ordination, as the leader and the people have had years of experience supporting one another in living their baptismal vows. The local congregation is presenting "one of their own" to the bishop to be ordained to a new role. The acclamation by the congregation: "He [or she] is worthy!" is clearly from the heart and carries much weight. There is no question about mutuality and continuity within the life of the local congregation. The action of the bishop and the participation of those from other congregations add a dimension of continuity with the church universal to the new relationship being forged by the Holy Spirit between these persons locally.

A service of "welcoming" or "induction" of a new minister will primarily be necessary when a congregation is calling as leaders those who have *not* been ordained or commissioned locally, when these leaders are being "imported" rather than emerging naturally from the local community. The bishop is present to assert his or her affirmation of the new minister's role in this community and the connectedness of that person's ministry to the bishop's, hence to the church universal. But, in addition, there is a need to establish a mutual pastoral relationship between the new minister and this congregation. The presenting crisis is that these people have no "track record" together. They have not lived together long enough for the people to be able to assert *from their own experience* that: "This person is a leader *for us*, one who speaks for us and represents who we are and what we are about." What, then, is an authentic role for the congregation under these circumstances?

Consider another moment in the life of a congregation when a new member is welcomed who has not had a lengthy history in that congregation: the baptism of an infant. It is expected that sufficient effort is extended toward the parents and sponsors of the infant to prepare them for their role in supporting the baptismal life of the child. The congregation is also involved significantly in the process of preparation (*catechesis*) and continuing support (*mystagogy*). Still, even without a lengthy period of preparation of the infant-candidate him or herself, we can baptize with confidence for several reasons. First, this new birth in Christ is accomplished by the action of the Holy Spirit, not by our response to that action. Certainly, we take seriously our responsibility to support the spiritual life of the newly baptized, but it is not our actions alone that make the sacramental action "valid." Rather, we rely upon the action of the Holy Spirit to accomplish what we fail to complete.

Second, we assume that this child will be learning and growing as he or she participates in the life and mission of the church in the years to come. It doesn't all have to happen before the actual baptism, as long as we continue the process of "formation" in the years that follow.

Third, in the case of the baptism of an infant, great emphasis is placed upon the intention and commitment of the parents and sponsors—indeed, of the entire congregation. In many congregations, the question: "Is this candidate prepared to receive this sacrament?" is being voiced in the same breath with another question: "Are *we* prepared, as a community of faith, to administer this sacrament?" The inclusion in the baptismal liturgy of a renewal of baptismal vows for all who have just promised "to support these persons in their life in Christ" addresses this concern. It is a serious, if also a joyful, business to baptize. The sponsors and witnessing congregation are assuming at least as much responsibility as the candidates themselves, for the integrity of the life of the local congregation (the context for the spiritual growth of the newly baptized) is vital to effective support of these persons. *"It takes a village to raise a child,"* the African proverb declares!

Returning to this liturgy of welcoming a new member (this time a "new minister") to the life and ministry of a congregation: the liturgy should rehearse the role of the entire congregation in the mutual life and mission they will share. It is appropriate that all the baptized be recalled to their role in supporting the life and mission of the congregation, responsibility which the new minister will now share with them. This makes plain to everyone that the new minister is here not to replace but to support the continuing ministry and leadership of those who now greet him or her!

But another question emerges. In his contribution to this collection, William Seth Adams asks us to consider how things might be different in the church if our ecclesiology was formed on baptism, not ordination. He suggests that we view ourselves as standing primarily in "the blessed company of all faithful people," rather than exclusively in the company of "the successors of the apostles."[4] If we are to accept baptism as the foundation of our understanding of church, we must consider how our (ordained) leaders relate to all the baptized. Can we, should we, be speaking of this "new minister" as we speak of any other member? In what way is our relationship with this person different from our relationship with others?

The Puzzle of the Relationship of the Baptized to Their Leaders

> Jesus called the disciples and said to them, "You know that among the Gentiles those whom they recognize as their rulers lord it over them, and their great ones are tyrants over them. But it is not so among you; but whoever wishes to become great among you must be your servant, and whoever wishes to be first among you must be slave of all. For the Son of Man came not to be served but to serve, and to give his life as a ransom for many." (Mark 10:42-45)

Let the elders who rule well be considered worthy of double honor, especially those who labor in preaching and teaching, for the scripture says, "You shall not muzzle an ox while it is treading out the grain." (1 Timothy 5:17-18)

There has always been some degree of tension within the life of the church as to the appropriate relationship between leaders and the rest of the community of the faithful. Leaders significantly represent us and recall us to those aspects of our life together which are central. Were we to arrange our lives around a romantic notion that we need have no leaders, in fact, leaders would emerge anyway, perhaps wielding power in inappropriate ways. Clearly, we wish to embrace the ministry of leadership in the church and incorporate that ministry into our life together in ways that do not inhibit, but rather promote, powerful participation by all members in the common life of the community.

In a wonderful discussion of these issues, *Being Clergy, Staying Human: Taking Our Stand in the River,* Dorothy McRae-McMahon points out that it is easy to think that the clergy's role is about being called to "heroism," being experts in every aspect of church life, "extra-special" people. An obsessive pursuit of such a role can easily destroy both cleric and congregation. Instead, McRae-McMahon prefers to draw an image for the role of leadership in the Church from a passage in Joshua (Joshua 3:6,8). The people of Israel are waiting on the banks of the Jordan River to enter the Promised Land. Joshua says to the priests, "Lift up the ark of the covenant and pass in front of the people." Then God tells Joshua to tell the priests that when they come to the edge of the waters of the Jordan, they are to take their stand in the river. Leaders in the church, says McRae-McMahon, are those who take the initiative to "step first into the river," to show others what can be done, to encourage them to follow.[5]

While I do not agree that it should *always* be the *ordained* who are "the first to step into the river," I do believe that the primary call of any church leader is to live and act with personal integrity and courage. What leaders stand for, and *where* they stand, affects the entire congregational system. Sometimes a leader will take the first step him or herself. Other times he or she will be supporting others as they make their move. In either case, the effectiveness of leadership is judged by whether the presence and activity of the leader(s) issue in more participation by all the baptized in the ministry of Christ.

By baptism, all share in the eternal priesthood and servanthood of Christ, but some stand among us as "signs" of these things. What does that mean? A sign is that which points to a reality beyond itself, participating to some extent in that reality, but not exhausting that reality. The gift of a wedding ring, for example, is a sign of love shared in a relationship, a reminder of that love. It is not in and of itself all that is loving in the relationship. It does not exhaust the couple's love. But it is, to some extent, also a source of that which it signifies. *Gifts cause what they signify to take place.* The giving of a wedding ring is both a sign of love shared and the occasion of more love being generated. In the act of the giving of the ring, more love is added to the relationship.

We can speak of ordination as a gift to the church so that the church can be a gift to the world. The deacon, for example, points toward and reminds us of the call of all the baptized to participate in the servanthood, the *diakonia,* of Christ. The deacon does not exhaust the ministry of servanthood in and of him or herself, but, if effective in that ministry, causes more of that which the office signifies to take place: more participation by all the baptized in the servanthood of Christ. The deacon, then, is one of the leaders of the diaconal ministry of the congregation, who stands among those leaders to remind all the baptized of the ministry in which they all share. In doing this, he or she causes more participation in that ministry to take place.[6]

A liturgy for welcoming new ministers should recognize not only the work to be pursued by that individual, but also the ministry *signified* by that minister's role or order (if ordained) and how the entire community of the baptized participates therein.

The Mystery of Continuity

The arrival of a "new minister" also raises the issue of *continuity* in the life of the congregation. At a time of transition, many are asking: will this continue to be the same congregation for me? Will our local traditions continue to be honored? How will this new chapter in our congregation's life be connected to what has gone before?

In Anglicanism, one sign of the mystery of continuity is the tradition of "apostolic succession" through ordination. Ignatius of Antioch described the bishop as a sign of unity and continuity within the eucharistic assembly. Irenaeus saw the bishop as providing unity of apostolic teaching; Cyprian taught that the bishop unified the local church community with the church universal. Ordination of leaders in a local community celebrates connectedness with the larger church in all these ways, but that is only one way in which continuity and coherence are achieved through ordination. Ordination also celebrates a continuity that exists internally for a community: continuity with its own unique local history and tradition. This is why it has always been essential that a candidate for ordination be presented to the bishop by the people as one whom they affirm as a leader. Relationship to a local community is essential to the regularity of the sacrament of ordination.

Thus we need both bishop and local congregational leaders to take significant roles liturgically at a "Celebration of a New Ministry." The bishop, in conferring authority upon the new minister(s) to function in that community (specifically by the reading of the "Letter of Institution"), is rehearsing the continuity between this community and the church universal. But the affirmation of the new minister's authority by the local community is equally important. This new minister will stand among the continuing leaders of this congregation as a sign of the ministry which they all share. If the leader is seen as a focus of church unity, it is unity both locally and with the church universal. Both the tradition of the church universal *and* local church tradition need to be preserved and handed on.

This last point is often overlooked in considering the work of passing on the tradition of the church. In an illuminating discussion of this issue, Robert J. Schreiter describes how through the ages local church communities have wrestled with a tension: how to be faithful both to the contemporary, local experience of the Gospel and to the tradition of Christian life that has been received, "the deposit of the faith."[7] This tension is obvious when Christianity encounters extremely diverse cultures, but it is true of the encounter between "the great Christian tradition" and any local Christian community, in that every congregation can be understood to possess its own distinctive culture, norms, traditions and values.[8]

For tradition to have power, Schreiter asserts, it must have credibility, intelligibility, and authority for those who share it. In order for tradition to have life and breath, it must be received and appropriated by a local community, or it is lost. Thus we can speak of a conversation between "the great Christian tradition" and local experience, in which the action and reflection of the local community is at least as important as the work of those designated officially as "bearers of the tradition" of the church.

These insights herald a radical shift in the roles of the "professional theologian" and "the people" in the life of the church. Rather than being seen as the primary source of theological information or authority, the professional theologian serves as an important resource, "helping the community clarify its own experience and relate it to the experience of other communities, past and present." The theologian has an indispensable but limited role of "creating the bonds of mutual accountability between local and world Church."[9] Members of the local congregation, ordained or not, must be seen not as empty receptacles to be filled with the theological truth dispensed by experts, but as partners in the theological dialogue. As Ian M. Fraser puts it:

The proper subject-matter for theological reflection is [not] the preoccupations of the Church...the proper "reflectors" are [not] academically trained specialists, as if God had not equipped a body of people with gifts of the Spirit for discerning and expressing his will. ...People in the thick of life, struggling to make sense of it in complex, difficult/hopeful situations, who search the scriptures together as a source of light, have the equipment to do theology. They have to learn to do so, and be given confidence to do so.[10]

The local leaders of a Christian community, then, require a relationship of continuity with the larger church, acted out in this liturgy by the presence of the bishop. But the "new minister" must also clearly share authority and credibility locally to be effective in "bearing" or "handing on" the tradition. Otherwise he or she may actually inhibit, rather than promote, the preservation of church tradition! Opportunity for the community to commit itself to helping the new minister(s) establish such local credibility is of utmost importance at this time.

"It Takes a Village..."

Our discussion of the mystery of continuity, then, leads to the mystery of mutuality. If *"it takes a village to raise a child,"* it also "takes a village" to establish effective leadership, continuity, and courageous innovation in the life of any congregation. Ministry is exercised by the entire community of faith. The participation of each and every member, including the "new minister," is essential to its effectiveness. The new minister will play a significant role in the life and mission of the congregation not by replacing people in their ministries, but by helping them to share ever more powerfully in the leadership of the congregation. A "Celebration of a New Ministry" is not an occasion of people gathering to proclaim hope and faith in what the new minister can do among these "his or her new people." Rather, it should be an occasion of an entire community gathering to proclaim faith and hope in what Christ is already doing among them. The mystery is not just that Christ can work through the ministry of those ordained or designated as "new ministers," but that Christ can and does work through the ministry of *all* the baptized! And when we have that in focus, a far more honest and healthy relationship emerges between those who lead and all other members of the Body.

It is essential that leaders in the church not define their entire identity and sense of self-worth in relation to their formal role within the institution. When clergy or other church leaders forget that they share an identity and common life with all the baptized, they lose perspective. When one is caught in a set of relationships within the church in which mutuality is replaced with a one-way, "trickle-down" flow of information or spiritual nurturing, not only is our life together diminished, it is, in fact, dangerous to the leader's own spiritual life.

Instead, church leaders need to be recalled to the roots of their Christian lives: that their highest calling is the same as that of anyone baptized, that is, *to live with integrity in response to their own baptismal vows.* All sacraments, including ordination, are but occasions for this response to baptism.

Many seem to have the impression that the professional church leader is somehow diminished when all the baptized are empowered to share more powerfully in the leadership of the church. The mystery of mutuality is that the opposite is the case. For whenever anyone in the Body of Christ is empowered to act more boldly, with more personal authority, *every* member is honored and strengthened. Never is the seminary-trained professional more valued and useful than when a local community is filled with people who are empowered to preach and teach and engage in every facet of the ministry of the church and, even more significantly, engaged in powerful witness and service in every component of their daily lives!

Clearly we need to avoid the notion that the "new minister" has arrived to "deliver ministry services" to congregants, the passive consumers. Perhaps it is also time to move beyond the idea that the professional church leader is to "develop" the ministries of the others. Instead, let us remember that in our spiritual friendship, it is Christ who is "developing" each of our baptismal ministries. It is a two-way relationship in which both "new minister" and congregants discover their ministries further "developed" in the context of their life together. Those with graduate education bring that education into the conversation, not to replace dialogue with pronouncement, but rather to listen first and then respond. With such humility, the received tradition will be far more effectively heard and incorporated into people's lives. "To each is given a manifestation of the Spirit for the common good" (I Cor. 12:7), and as *all* share what they have been given, each grows in faith.

It is important that the new minister be recognized not only as a leader, but also as a companion in faith, in need of pastoral ministry from the congregation as well as a dispenser of the same. Dorothy McRae-McMahon, who, as discussed earlier, takes as an image for church leadership "stepping first into the river," writes:

> I think the time has come to lay aside the saint and martyr images which are largely oppressive and unattractive, and to dare to lead the way into authentic humanness. ... "And so," I ask myself, "could it be that the bravest and truest way to lead people into life is to be authentically human ourselves?" ... Experience has shown me that the world is waiting for a human Church—where people can be honest with one another, in which leaders give clear evidence of going through universal human struggles.[11]

It is, in fact, a gift to the entire congregation when leaders share their personal struggles appropriately with other baptized members of the congregation. To maintain a false *persona* as one who never struggles is a disservice to the congregation, by promoting a standard for Christian living which is both unrealistic and ultimately unfaithful because it is born of fear of how we will be received if we appear less than perfect.

"It takes a village to raise a new minister," for the entire community plays a role in affirming and responding to the new minister as a leader. Continuing local leaders who already possess local authority and credibility, who already have the trust and confidence of the local community, will need to invite the newcomer into relationship with them and establish a collegial and mutually supportive spiritual friendship. To hold the new minister off at a distance, as if the substance of his or her spiritual life were of a different character than their own, will leave the new minister starving for spiritual support. To hang back, waiting for the new minister to take the lead rather than continuing to pursue their ministry with spirit and zeal, will only leave the new minister to make misinformed choices, regularly frustrating the needs and expectations of others. Instead, the new minister needs direct and honest feedback, and to be invited to engage in community life, not only in his or her official role, but also as a fellow person of faith in search of spiritual and personal support. The new minister, of course, also needs to embrace the assertiveness of other leaders in the congregation, rather than trying to orchestrate everyone's every move.

When I moved to the Diocese of Northern Michigan just over a year ago from New York (where I had received my primary formation in baptism and ordination), it was clear to me that I needed "catechesis" from people here. I knew what it meant to be Christian and Episcopalian in New York and how to be a "Rector" in a conventional sense. But now I was to serve as a "Missioner," supporting the development of ministry in a number of small, remote communities where people are taking responsibility for their own life and mission, rather than relying predominantly upon help coming in "from outside." I needed to learn what it meant *for them* to be Christian and to participate in the life of the church in their communities. I needed people to act, as it were, as "sponsors," praying with me, sharing their stories of how the Holy

Spirit had been and still was active in the lives of their congregations. I needed to learn the local traditions, even, at times, the language! (What is a "Yooper" or a "Pastie" or a "Troll"?) In the congregations I serve, it is clear that my leadership and capacity to serve are strengthened where that ministry of "catechesis" is taken seriously. In the communities which assumed that I was arriving with all the expertise, that they were there to be formed by me (with little mutuality in the process), in those places I find my presence and activity far less effective. Imported leaders, even those with a seminary education and years of experience, need *catechesis* by the communities in which they serve, just as surely as do those being baptized.

In fact, those of us who have spent the bulk of our adult lives (starting at an early age) being called "Father" or "Mother" by people of obviously deeper maturity and spiritual depth, know how powerfully all the baptized *do* minister to their leaders. This is done in so many ways: by example of Christian living, by gentle questioning, or by bold and prophetic action.

Jean Haldane has pointed out that it is not that our members are reluctant to minister until clergy talk them into it. Mature, responsible adults are already engaged in significant ministry all the time! Rather, so much of the ministry which members pursue is undervalued or ignored by the church. She writes:

> The Church offers warmth of relationship, common purpose, and a chance to do those neighborly things we find difficult in society. In contrast, laity's ministry in the world is complex, often difficult and unclear. Many experience struggles of conscience, tensions and worry in their work, loneliness in the gray areas of public conduct and practice. So, they collude with the clergy to keep themselves focused within church programs.[12]

How easy it is to steer church program toward those issues and matters in which the seminary–trained clergy have expertise, deftly avoiding the thorny issues with which most members are truly struggling. Leaders in the church who spend too many waking hours on "church work" need help in lifting their vision to issues with which others in the community are also concerned. When church members refuse to allow the church to devote so much time, energy and resources internally, then their leaders are truly being ministered to by their brothers and sisters in Christ.

"Mutuality" involves all members of the congregation asserting their insights and concerns and questions into the fabric of church life, so that the entire faith community is called out of narcissistic self-absorption into fuller participation in the life of the world. It is essential, then, that a rite which celebrates a new chapter in the life and ministry of a congregation (marked by the arrival of new clergy) proclaim the many dimensions of the ministry in which all the baptized are engaged.

Reflections on the "Celebration of a New Ministry"

The occasion of the "Celebration of a New Ministry" might be used to raise such issues within a congregation as it prepares to welcome new leaders. A "Celebration Committee," representative of the congregation, including continuing congregational leaders and the new minister, could meet to discuss the shape and message of the service. Here are some issues which might be considered:

What Is the Purpose of This Liturgy?

The new minister, ordained or not, has been called by the people for a special purpose. They are gathering to welcome this person as a companion in faith, as well as to recognize him or her formally as a leader among them. A new, mutual pastoral relationship is being established between them.

Increasingly, congregations are choosing different patterns of ministry. Many continue to pursue a "one-priest, one-parish" model, but work collegially with a team of persons sharing formally in leadership ("lay pastors," deacons, locally ordained persons, and so on). Others choose to participate in "clusters" or regional ministries, led by ministry teams. Alterations in the service need to be made accordingly. When it involves a "multi-point" setting, for example, provision should be made for involvement of all congregations and persons who are engaged in the ministry which the new minister is joining.

While the arrival of the new leader marks a turning point in their life together, the local community has a history rich with its own traditions and customs which ought to be considered when planning the celebration. Work which has gone before and work which is continuing ought to be acknowledged. Continuing leaders who function regularly liturgically should be included as much as possible in those roles, so that continuity within this local community of faith is affirmed. The new minister will be supporting, not replacing, the ministry and continuing leadership of those who now greet him or her.

The Title of the Service:

When we speak of a "Celebration of a New Ministry," what exactly is being celebrated? Is it the new position of a professional cleric (his or her latest "career move")? Certainly not! Is it the ministry of the entire congregation that is now considered "new"? While there is definite newness in the life of this congregation with the arrival of a new leader, the essential ministry of the congregation is continuing in the ministry of the people of that place. Let us assume that the ministry of this congregation remains strong and vital, sturdy enough to welcome new leadership without having to be dismantled or scrapped to make it easier for the new minister to adapt.

With these thoughts in mind, some congregations have chosen to call this service: "A CELEBRATION OF THE LIFE AND MISSION OF [_____]CHURCH, AT THE INDUCTION OF [_____] AS [RECTOR]."

The Entrance:

Too often, the entrance to this rite is orchestrated like an ordination, built around the person and new status of the ordinand: processing in a place of special honor, surrounded by special ministers and sponsors. Clergy are set apart, processing in vestments, then sitting in a prominent location, to support a colleague on his or her new beginning. But this service is not an ordination. It is the establishing of a new, mutual pastoral relationship between people of faith as they begin to pursue ministry together. Unfortunately, the structure of the existing service, opening as it does with "The Institution," encourages the parallel between the opening of this service and an ordination. Perhaps a "Celebration Committee" could reflect upon how to arrange the entrance to communicate the collegial dimension of the relationship between the new minister and those continuing in roles of leadership in the congregation.

The Institution:

It is important at this service to affirm the connectedness of this new minister to both the bishop and the local congregation. Preceding the reading of the Letter of Institution, the Warden might read a brief letter of agreement between the new minister and the Vestry which states plainly, in their own words, the nature of the relationship and the duties which this new minister is assuming. This would affirm the role of the local congregation in establishing the authority of the new minister to function locally, just as the bishop is affirming the authority of the new minister to act on his or her behalf. It would also be in order for the Vestry to review carefully the Letter of Institution (BCP, p. 557) to ensure that it is consonant with their understanding of this person's role among them. Both letters should be discussed with the bishop well in advance to address any questions or concerns they may raise.

If it has been decided to play down the connection between ordination and this gathering, consider replacing the "Litany for Ordinations" with a different litany, such as the Prayers of the People provided in *Supplemental Liturgical Texts (Prayer Book Studies 30)*. These underscore the essential involvement of all the baptized in the ministry of the church, a good theme to recall at this moment in the liturgy.[13] The "Celebration Committee" may wish to work with the new minister(s) to write their own litany. Be sure to include a petition for all the world, not just this congregation. It is essential at this moment that we be reminded that as grand as all this may be, we *are* called to a life and mission beyond the church walls as well!

Consider whether the collect following the litany (BCP, p. 560) describes the relationship intended between the new minister and the congregation. Does the "patience and understanding," the "love and care," flow only one way in this relationship? Perhaps the collect used after the litany at ordinations (BCP, p. 515; cf. pp. 528, 540) might be substituted.

The Liturgy of the Word:

In addition to the lessons listed on p. 560 in the Prayer Book, you may wish to consider Exodus 19:3-8; Isaiah 61:1-8; Psalm 40, 121, 15, or 34:1-8; 1 Peter 2:4-10; 1 Peter 4:7-11; Acts 6:1-7; or Mark 10:35-45.

The Induction:

Consider what is happening here. Symbols are being presented to the new minister to recognize the nature of the ministry and the mutual pastoral relationship being established between these people. For symbols to be given exclusively to the new minister may send the message that "We are handing over the ministries of this congregation to you. *Here: now you do it!*" We want to recognize the new minister's gifts of leadership and function according to the order in which he or she is ordained, but it should be done in a way that reminds us that there will be a sharing of leadership here. In effect, we might think of this moment as installing the new minister into a new position: standing *among* the continuing congregational leaders. When others will share directly in the leadership of the ministry represented by a symbol, they could stand with the new minister as the symbol is presented. This would rehearse the mutuality and collegiality of leadership, and the fact that the new minister has come to support, not replace, the continuing ministries and leadership of the persons who now greet him or her.

Instead of giving the symbols directly to the new minister, consider having them placed where the community will be using them: the Bible on the lectern, the water poured into the baptismal font, oil presented to the new minister standing with others who will be sharing in a healing ministry, the bread and wine placed upon the altar.[14] Remember that all symbols should be large enough to be visible to all (e.g., using a sizable flagon of baptismal water) and should remain in the sight of the congregation during the Induction. The vestments and bread and wine may be used in the Eucharist which follows (see BCP, p. 565).

Some congregations have experimented with having both the new minister and other leaders of the congregation receive symbols to affirm and authenticate their various roles in ministry. In some places, the new minister him or herself has made some of the presentations. It works best when this is done in a manner that clearly proclaims how the new minister will relate to those persons and their work. Those engaged in various ministries should consider carefully which symbols to present, so that the items presented are not trivial but point toward and participate in a greater reality. Reflect carefully upon what is being said by each symbol, who gives it and who receives it. If you were visiting or new to the Episcopal Church, would it be clear to you what is happening here and what is the nature of the relationship being established?

In some places, words have been added to rehearse the share of the entire congregation in these continuing ministries.[15] Consider this alternative:

(Bible)   N., the ministry we share is founded in and upon God's Holy Word.

All: *Join us in proclaiming the Word of God.*

Or: *Support us as together we proclaim the Word of God.*

(Water) N., it is our privilege and responsibility to share the Good News of Christ with all people of God's creation, that they might be restored to unity with God and each other in Christ.

All: *Join us in baptizing in obedience to our Lord.*

(Priest's Stole) [*if a priest*]

N., in baptism we were anointed by the Holy Spirit that we might all participate in Christ's eternal priesthood.

All: *[Stand among us as a priest and] join us in being pastors one to another.*

(Deacon's Stole) [*if a vocational deacon*]

N., in baptism we were anointed by the Holy Spirit that we might all participate in the servanthood of Christ.

All: *[Stand among us as a deacon and] join us in being servants of Christ in the world.*

(Prayer Book)

N., the apostle Paul reminds us that we are to pray unceasingly.

All: *Join us in offering the prayer of Christ [daily in this place].*

(Oil)   N., Jesus came among us to bring healing and wholeness to our broken world.

All: *Join us in being healers and reconcilers in Christ's name.*

(Keys)   N., this church building stands as a symbol of Christ's presence in the midst of our world.

All: *Join us in opening the doors of this place to all people.*

(Canons) N., as members of the Body of Christ, we are responsible to and interdependent with one another.

All: *Join us in obeying these Canons and sharing in the councils of this diocese.*

(Bread and Wine)

N., in the Eucharist, we gather constantly to be nourished and sent forth in ministry.

All: *Join us in the breaking of the bread, as we offer our gifts in praise and thanksgiving to God.*

Such statements will need to be adapted depending upon the circumstances. A towel might be presented as a symbol of servanthood, for example, if the new minister is not ordained a vocational deacon. If the new minister will serve in a specific role, the words accompanying these presentations should make that clear. But it should be equally clear how others will be sharing in that work.

The opportunity for other symbols to be added (BCP, p. 561) could be used creatively:

* to affirm the ministries of members of the congregation as they are pursued in their daily lives, clarifying how the new minister will be involved in supporting them in that work;
* to involve children in the liturgy;
* to affirm local history and customs;
* to acknowledge the work of those who have gone before and those who will continue as leaders in ministry in this community;
* to recognize the ministry in which the new minister was engaged previously, perhaps including a presentation from the community of faith which the new minister has just left;
* to involve representatives of other religious bodies and community organizations;
* to acknowledge the work of the Search Committee and of interim pastors and consultants.

For the prayer following the presentations: Consider whether it would be appropriate to have the new minister lead the congregation in prayer, rather than pray by him or herself. In that case, a prayer such as the Prayer of St. Francis (BCP, p. 833) might be appropriate.

Prayer After Communion:

Consider as an alternative to the prayer on p. 564:

> Almighty Father, we thank you for feeding us with the holy food of the Body and Blood of your Son, and for uniting us through him in the fellowship of your Holy Spirit. We thank you for calling us to be a ministering community in your redeemed world, and for raising up among us faithful servants for your ministry. We pray that we may be to one another effective examples in

word and action, in love and patience, and in holiness of life. Grant that we may serve you now, and always rejoice in your glory; through Jesus Christ your Son our Lord, who lives and reigns with you and the Holy Spirit, one God, now and for ever. Amen.

NOTES

1. The term "vacant congregation" is often used to describe a congregation without a rector or vicar. Use of this term demeans the presence and ministry of the laity, who have not left the congregation "vacant" but remain active and vital members.

2. Josephine Borgeson and Lynne Wilson, eds., *Reshaping Ministry*, Chapter 1.

3. Some of these ideas were explored in the address of Richard Norris to the 1984 Trinity Institute Symposium on the Mission of the Church.

4. See above, p. 5.

5. Dorothy McRae-McMahon, *Being Clergy, Staying Human: Taking Our Stand in the River*, pp. vii-2.

6. Many of these ideas were developed by Bishop Richard Grein in addresses to the clergy of the Diocese of New York in 1991.

7. Robert J. Schreiter, *Constructing Local Theologies*, p. xi.

8. For more on this see James F. Hopewell, *Congregation: Stories and Structures*.

9. Schreiter, p. 18.

10. Ian M. Fraser, *Reinventing Theology: As the People's Work*, p. 9.

11. McRae-McMahon, p. 3.

12. Jean Haldane, "Toward a Totally Ministering Church," *Crossings* (Church Divinity School of the Pacific, Winter, 1987), p. 4.

13. For example, petitions in the Prayers of the People—First Supplement ask that God "strengthen, bless, and guide us to make you [God] known by word and example," and "guide and bless us in our work and in our play,...that all people may share in the fulfillment of your creative work." In the Second Supplement, the prayer for the church remembers "particularly all the baptized who minister in this congregation and community." See *Supplemental Liturgical Texts*, Prayer Book Studies 30 (New York: Church Hymnal, 1989), pp. 77-81.

14. This practice is suggested in "Celebration of a New Ministry," in *Occasional Celebrations* of the Anglican Church of Canada.

15. Liturgies included in the Total Ministry Notebook developed by the Episcopal Diocese of Nevada during the episcopate of Wesley Frensdorff contain examples of this.

BIBLIOGRAPHY

Allen, Roland. *Missionary Methods: St. Paul's or Ours?* Grand Rapids, MI: Eerdmans, 1962.

Anglican Church of Canada. *Occasional Celebrations.* Toronto: Anglican Book Centre, 1992.

Baptism, Eucharist and Ministry. Faith & Order Paper No. 111. Geneva: World Council of Churches, 1982.

The Book of Occasional Services. New York: Church Hymnal, 1991.

Borgeson, Josephine, and Wilson, Lynne, eds. *Reshaping Ministry: Essays in Memory of Wesley Frensdorff.* Arvada, CO: Jethro Publications, 1990.

Donovan, Vincent J. *Christianity Rediscovered.* Maryknoll, NY: Orbis Books, 1978.

Episcopal Diocese of Nevada. *Total Ministry Notebook.* 1985.

Fraser, Ian M. *Reinventing Theology: As the People's Work.* Glasgow: Wild Goose Publications, 1988.

Haldane, Jean. "Toward a Totally Ministering Church." In *Crossings* (Church Divinity School of the Pacific, Winter, 1987).

Hopewell, James F. *Congregation: Stories and Structures.* Philadelphia: Fortress, 1987.

McRae-McMahon, Dorothy. *Being Clergy, Staying Human: Taking Our Stand in the River.* Washington, DC: Alban Institute, 1992.

Mead, Loren. *The Once and Future Church: Reinventing the Congregation for a New Mission Frontier.* Washington, DC: Alban Institute, 1991.

Merriman, Michael W., ed. *The Baptismal Mystery and the Catechumenate.* New York: Church Hymnal, 1990.

Norris, Richard. "Baptism, Christian Identity and the Mission of the Church," Address to the Trinity Institute Symposium on the Mission of the Church, 1984. Tapes available from The Episcopal Radio-TV Foundation, Inc., 3379 Peachtree Road, N.E., Atlanta, GA 30326.

Pobee, John S. "Spectrum of Ministry," in *Ministry Formation,* January, 1993. World Council of Churches, Unit I: Unity and Renewal.

Schreiter, Robert J. *Constructing Local Theologies.* Maryknoll, NY: Orbis Books, 1985.

Schillebeeckx, Edward. *The Church with the Human Face.* New York: Crossroad, 1985.

The Reaffirmation of Ordination Vows

The Reverend Michael W. Hopkins

In the opening essay of this collection, William Seth Adams makes the case for an ecclesiology built on a "baptismal paradigm." He is critical of the church's current practice of ordination rites that overshadows the baptismal rite and argues, effectively, for a reformation of practice that would put baptism in its appropriate position of primacy. Such a reformation is essential for a baptismal paradigm to replace what Paul Avis calls the "apostolic paradigm" that tends "to make the life of the whole body dependent upon one particular instrument of that life—[ordained] ministry."[1]

As Adams suggests, it is characteristic of the current state of liturgical reform that there is an incongruence between the ritual texts (as we have them in The Book of Common Prayer) and the ritual actions, environment, and interpretive framework within which these texts exist and are used. This incongruence has not allowed the texts "to tell the whole truth." There is also an incoherence between the rite of baptism and (as Adams puts it) "other rites in the complex." I wish to explore this latter notion further, with direct application to the current practice of the "Reaffirmation of Ordination Vows."

A form for the "Reaffirmation of Ordination Vows" is found in *The Book of Occasional Services.*[2] It is one example of a new class of rites that have become relatively popular. These rites allow for occasions of reaffirmation or renewal of otherwise non-repeatable sacramental rites (i.e., Baptism, Ordination, and Marriage). Thus we have in The Book of Common Prayer the "Renewal of

Baptismal Vows," the "Reaffirmation of Baptismal Vows" as part of the rite of Confirmation, and "A Form of Commitment to Christian Service" (which provides for the occasion being a "renewal" and always includes a "reaffirmation of baptismal promises").[3] In *The Book of Occasional Services* we have the "Anniversary of a Marriage,"[4] besides the "Reaffirmation of Ordination Vows." Provision is also made for the reaffirmation of the promises of episcopal ordination at the investiture of a diocesan bishop.[5]

The purpose of this paper is fourfold: to suggest a way of understanding the sacraments that is rooted in the Anglican tradition, to explore the relationship of these rites of reaffirmation with the sacraments themselves, to evaluate the rite for the "Reaffirmation of Ordination Vows" and its current use within the church, and to make four proposals based on this discussion.

A Way of Understanding the Sacraments

The Chicago-Lambeth Quadrilateral includes as one of the four essentials to Christian unity "The two Sacraments ordained by Christ Himself—Baptism and the Supper of the Lord."[6] The primacy of these two sacraments has been a foundational part of the Anglican tradition from its earliest days. The Articles of Religion maintain the distinction between the "two Sacraments ordained of Christ our Lord in the Gospel" and the "five commonly called Sacraments" that "are not to be counted for Sacraments of the Gospel."[7]

I believe that this distinction continues to be important and that any understanding of the sacraments, the liturgy of the church taken as a whole, as well as the ministry to which all Christians are called that is essentially formed by this liturgy, must begin here. Here, I too am persuaded, like Adams, that "the ritual life of a community is formative of that community."[8]

The Prayer Book calls Baptism "full initiation by water and the Holy Spirit into Christ's Body the Church." Furthermore, the bond God establishes in this initiation is described as "indissolu-ble." The Eucharist is described as "the principal act of Christian worship on the Lord's Day and other major Feasts."[9] Baptism ini-tiates one into a community whose regular act of worship is the Eucharist. Indeed the newly baptized first act upon initiation by participation in the Eucharist.

Baptism is "indissoluble." It is never repeated. What is repeated is participation in the Eucharist, where the community re-gathers and re-presents the story into which all are baptized, that is, the death and resurrection of Christ. In the same spirit of understand-ing these two Sacraments as "of the Gospel" and therefore essential to the full life of the church, I would suggest that Baptism and Eucharist constitute the essential initiation into the life of Christ and constant renewal of that life, respectively. All "other sacramen-tal rites" and ritual acts must depend upon the "Sacraments of the Gospel" for their meaning. As Adams suggests must be true of ordination in relationship to baptism,[10] all other sacramental rites must also point to the Gospel Sacraments as the principal and essential ordering of the church's ministry and renewal.

Within this scheme, "confirmation," as we have it in The Book of Common Prayer 1979, is itself the first occasion of mature pub-lic renewal of the baptismal covenant in the presence of a bishop. Whether the provision for reception and reaffirmation makes con-firmation repeatable is open for debate. I believe it does. I would argue that the "non-repeatable" aspect of historic confirmation is now contained in the rite of Baptism, i.e., the prayer for the gifts of the Spirit and consignation with optional anointing with chrism.[11] The appearance of "non-repeatability" has been main-tained by allowing for only one "confirmation," which may then be followed by "reaffirmation(s)." In reality, however, the differ-ence seems to be in name only, despite the rather weak form pro-vided for the bishop's prayer over the candidate for reaffirmation compared with that for confirmation.[12]

Reaffirmations and the Sacraments

Each of the new rites of reaffirmation is the renewal of an otherwise non-repeatable sacrament. They recognize the paradox implicit in each of those rites—the "already" of the gift of God and the "not yet" of our reception of and response to that gift. Each time of renewal is a time to recognize our need to live out God's call to us, to become who we already are in Christ through the indwelling of the Holy Spirit.

The danger in these rites of renewal is that they might overshadow the Gospel Sacraments themselves. Maintaining the proper perspective is important. The primacy of Baptism as the essential non-repeatable sacrament and the Eucharist as the essential repeatable sacrament must always be maintained. Baptism is always the expression of the *fullness* of our identity in Christ and of God's call to us to be the people of God. Ordination and Marriage are particular (and partial) expressions of that call. The Eucharist itself is the great sacrament of renewal, the food for our ongoing life as God's people. Nothing can replace the renewal that occurs when Eucharist is celebrated and God is reaffirmed as "God among us." The Eucharist is the primary occasion for baptismal renewal (and, therefore, for renewal of one's commitment to service, to one's ordination, or even to one's marriage).

A priority is thus seen first for the sacraments of Baptism and Eucharist and second for the renewal of the baptismal covenant within the context of the Eucharist. All other renewals are summed up in that renewal. To renew one's baptismal covenant is also to renew one's commitment to service, to one's ordination, or to one's marriage.

This is not to say that there are not occasions when it is appropriate and even important to reaffirm the more particular vows of, for instance, ordination. It is to say that such reaffirmations must remain firmly grounded in the church's baptismal and eucharistic life. If they do not, other sacramental rites take on a distorted importance. The context in which they are celebrated is, therefore, of vital importance.

The Reaffirmation of Ordination Vows: An Evaluation of Current Practice

A form for the Reaffirmation of Ordination Vows first appeared in *The Book of Occasional Services* in its first edition (1979). It had no predecessor in *The Book of Offices* (1960).

The rite has no solid historical precedence. It did not appear until 1970 when Pope Paul VI promulgated the new *Missale Romanum*. A form for the "Renewal of Priestly Vows" was inserted into the Chrism Mass of Holy Thursday on the advice, not of the Congregation of Divine Worship, but of the Congregation of the Clergy.[13] This was a new idea without precedent, except perhaps in the "modernist oath" required of all clergy in 1910 (which, however, was not placed in a liturgical context). The rite seems to have been a reaction to a series of events in the late 1960s. In 1967, Paul VI called for a renewed commitment to priestly celibacy. This was followed by the publication of *Humanae Vitae* in 1968 (with its ensuing turmoil) and the call for a married priesthood by the Dutch Pastoral Council in January 1970. Roman Catholics in both Europe and the United States received the new rite with some suspicion.[14]

The form for Reaffirmation of Ordination Vows in *The Book of Occasional Services* cites two occasions at which its use is appropriate: "at a celebration of the Eucharist upon an occasion when the clergy are gathered with the bishop," and "at the reception of a priest from another Communion or the restoration of a priest." The form proposes the possibility of its being used on Maundy Thursday, stating that, if it is, it should *not* be at the Proper Liturgy of the day. A Collect is provided along with suggested psalms and lessons. The rite itself includes an address by the bishop to the clergy, their response to four questions, and the bishop's own statement of reaffirmation. No role is given to the laity except (by implication) as witnesses. The bishop asks for a response to the questions "in the presence of Christ and his Church." The opening rubrics, however, suggest that the rite is intended to be an interaction largely between bishop and clergy.

The attraction to Maundy Thursday must first be questioned. Obviously the tie is to the institution of the Eucharist and (in the minds of some) to the institution of the priesthood. Two factors mitigate against this connection. First, since the rubrics do not allow reaffirmation at the Proper Liturgy of the day, the story of the Last Supper is not an optional reading at the Reaffirmation of Ordination Vows. More importantly, however, the "institution of the priesthood" in the events of the Last Supper is a tenuous theological proposition at best. Anglican tradition has always held that Christ instituted only Baptism and the Eucharist (the "Gospel Sacraments"). The presidency of the Eucharist granted to the ordained priesthood is a given of the tradition. To place the burden of its development on the story of the Last Supper, however, is problematic. Ordained priesthood as we know it developed over many centuries, and the notion that the priest celebrating the Eucharist takes the place of Christ at the Last Supper is unknown in the early church. Maundy Thursday is simply not the feast of the ordained priesthood.

Nonetheless, it has become popular to celebrate a Reaffirmation of Ordination Vows on Maundy Thursday or at some other time during Holy Week and to juxtapose this reaffirmation with the blessing of chrism. *The Book of Occasional Services* does not state explicitly whether or not this combination is a possibility. The "Consecration of Chrism Apart from Baptism" may be held at a separate service, but Maundy Thursday is not specifically suggested, as it is for the Reaffirmation of Ordination Vows. (Ironically there is historical precedence for the blessing of oils on Maundy Thursday.[15]) The propers provided in *The Book of Occasional Services* for a service at which chrism is consecrated apart from baptism emphasize the priesthood of Christ and the priesthood of all believers. Reaffirmation of Ordination Vows seems to cause some confusion in this setting. On the other hand, using the propers for Ordination or for the Celebration of a New Ministry at the Reaffirmation of Ordination Vows (as provided in *BOS*) and consecrating chrism is likewise confusing because the consecration formula for chrism asks that *all* who are sealed by this chrism might share in the eternal priesthood of Christ.[16] I will include a recommendation for the consecration of chrism at the end of this paper since it is tied to the Reaffirmation of Ordination Vows in so many dioceses.

This brings us to the next question, that of the presence and role of the laity. As it stands, the Reaffirmation of Ordination Vows does not conform to the liturgy to which it is fundamentally linked: ordination itself. Ordination cannot occur without the presence of the laity, who must be among those who present the candidates and who must give their assent to the act. More substantially, ordination clearly occurs within the context of the assembled church. The promises are made by the ordinand "in the presence of the Church" and the liturgy always occurs within the Eucharist.

Perhaps the problem here goes back one step further to what Adams calls the "ritual incoherence" between the ordination and baptismal rites. He asks, "What would an ordination rite look/feel like that saw itself as dependent upon and derivative from the baptismal rite?"[17] It might be conjectured that an ordination rite that was so dependent might produce a reaffirmation rite that was equally so. In other words, it seems as though the current Reaffirmation of Ordination Vows (especially in practice) highlights those aspects of the ordination rite that are especially incoherent with the baptismal rite. Some of the marks of incoherence that Adams cites serve as good examples: the celebration of ordination rites at special times with attendance by invitation; special entrance rites at ordinations that include the ordinand; special readings, preachers, and music; and the exclusively clerical focus of the "transitional moment," the consecration of the priest. Each of these tends to be true of the "Reaffirmation of Ordination Vows" as well. Moreover, in terms of the presence of the laity, the reaffirmation tends to exacerbate the lessened state of the laity evidenced at most ordinations.

Yet *The Book of Occasional Services* implies that reaffirmation might appropriately take place at such an event as a clergy conference. The integrity of such a setting, which all but excludes the presence of the laity, must be questioned. At the very least such a setting would greatly strain the phrase "in the presence of the Church." The same would be true if reaffirmation were to take place on Maundy Thursday morning or any other morning or afternoon during Holy Week. The availability of the laity (much less the clergy) at these times is minimal.

Clearly it is vital for the laity to be present at a reaffirmation of ordination vows. It is more than a reaffirmation of the relationship between the bishop and his or her clergy. It is a reaffirmation of the relationship between the clergy and the whole of Christ's church. This is not to say that the relationship between clergy and bishop is not important. It is to say that the relationship has no meaning outside the context of the whole people of God. One can say the same thing about ordained ministry in general. Ordained ministry has no meaning outside the ministry of the whole people of God. Ordination as a sacrament must find all its meaning in baptism, although, sadly, the ordination rite does not make this clear, and, in practice, ordination liturgies are much grander occasions than the average baptismal liturgy.

This raises the further question of the role of the laity in the Reaffirmation of Ordination Vows beyond their mere presence. If ministry is the province of the whole people of God, and if ordination itself is a particular form of this baptismal ministry, then it is questionable whether ordination vows should be renewed in isolation from this total ministry. To do so gives the appearance of clinging to an isolated model of ministry as primarily *ordained* ministry.

Reaffirming Ministry: Proposals

The following four proposals are made given the above discussion.

1. A Reaffirmation of Ministry that is inclusive of all the baptized (the whole ministry of the church) should be made available for significant diocesan occasions. At least two dioceses[18] currently have used such a rite at their annual diocesan convention, although both are evaluating whether this should be a yearly occurrence. It might be used only on specific occasions that themselves call for a special emphasis on the renewal of the ministry of the whole church.

2. Use of the "Reaffirmation of Ordination Vows" as it stands in *The Book of Occasional Services* would therefore be limited to the occasion of the reception of a priest from another Communion or of a restoration to the ministry. This limitation may call for revision of the rite itself, including a more specific title, a fuller set of questions, and an explicit declaration of reception or restoration.

3. Inclusion of some reaffirmation of ordination vows within the "Celebration of a New Ministry," as the most appropriate time for reaffirmation to occur. This follows the example of the Investiture of a new Diocesan Bishop. Provision should be made for such reaffirmation to be used also on the occasion of a major anniversary. In both cases, care must be taken to set the reaffirmation in the context of the baptismal ministry of the whole people of God.

4. The consecration of chrism is best reserved for episcopal visitations to congregations or some diocesan service that has baptism as its primary focus. A Maundy Thursday Consecration of Chrism has historical precedence, but one must ask the same question of it that must be asked of the Reaffirmation of Ordination Vows: What is its integrity without the presence of a significant body of laity? One can envision as a much more appropriate setting a diocesan celebra-

tion sometime during Lent at which those to be baptized at the coming Easter Vigil and their sponsors and catechists are present. Here the bishop could also exercise his or her role as chief catechist.

NOTES

1. *Anglicanism and the Christian Church* (Minneapolis: Fortress Press, 1989), p. 303.
2. *The Book of Occasional Services* (New York: Church Hymnal, 1991), p. 227. Hereinafter cited as *BOS* 1991.
3. BCP 1979, pp. 292, 413, and 420.
4. *BOS* 1991, p. 159.
5. Ibid., pp. 249-51.
6. BCP 1979, p. 878.
7. Ibid., p. 872.
8. See above, p. 12.
9. BCP 1979, pp. 298, 13.
10. See above, p. 13.
11. See, among others, the discussion in Gerard Austin, *The Rite of Confirmation: Anointing with the Spirit* (New York: Pueblo, 1985) and Daniel Stevick, *Baptismal Moments; Baptismal Meanings* (New York: Church Hymnal, 1987).
12. BCP 1979, pp. 418-419.
13. A 1969 letter from Cardinal Wright, prefect of the Congregation of the Clergy, urging such a rite, stated that it was desirable on Holy Thursday for every priest to renew the promise he had made to observe sacred celibacy and render obedience to his bishop.
14. See Neils Rasmussen, "The Chrism Mass: Tradition and Renewal," *The Cathedral Reader* (Washington: USCC Publications, 1979), pp. 29-33.

15. A "Chrism Mass" on Maundy Thursday first appeared in the Old Gelasian Sacramentary of the seventh century, a Roman Sacramentary with Frankish influences.

16. See *BOS* 1991, pp. 228-30, for the rite of "Consecration of Chrism Apart from Baptism."

17. See above, p. 13.

18. Washington and Western Michigan.

To Confirm or To Receive?

The Reverend Daniel B. Stevick

Baptized adults have, over the years, come to the Episcopal Church from other Christian communions in considerable numbers. For as long as anyone can remember, persons from Roman or Orthodox churches have been *received,* while those from Protestant communions have been sacramentally *confirmed.* The distinction in the manner of admitting newcomers from other churches is under question and in change in parts of the church, although in other places the matter has as of yet drawn little attention. This paper seeks to set forth some of the factors that must be taken into account when this practice of the Episcopal Church is rethought and customs are changed.

I.

Whether newcomers were received or were confirmed depended on whether or not their former churches had the historic episcopate. A consideration of this matter by the House of Bishops in 1937 (evidently the only judgment which might be thought to speak to the point with church-wide authority) concluded: "Persons who have received confirmation in the Roman Catholic Church, the Eastern Orthodox Church, the Old Catholic Church..., and the Reformed Episcopal Church may properly be received into the communion of the Episcopal Church without any additional laying on of hands." Their confirmation, like their baptism, should simply be recognized, not repeated.[1]

The statement went on to say that baptized persons from other churches, although they may have received a confirmation which was significant in their former communions, when they come into the Episcopal Church should "receive additional confirmation at the hands of a bishop." Their previous confirmation, unlike their baptism, was held to be denomination-specific. Even though it might go by the name "confirmation," it should not be equated with confirmation in the Episcopal Church.

Episcopacy was determinative. When someone in the House of Bishops debate questioned receiving persons from the Reformed Episcopal Church, reply was made, "Confirmation is by bishops, and that Church has the historic episcopate." Acceptable confirmation was taken to be coextensive with episcopacy.

II.

It is not clear when or why this distinction between the terms of admission for Catholics and Protestants became common practice. Until the late seventeenth century, the Church of England had little need to take account of other religious groups and to provide for changes in affiliation.

However, religious pluralism having become a fact of English society, in 1714 the Convocation of Canterbury issued a document for admitting converts from the Church of Rome or from "the separation." The form is penitential, especially for those who come from Rome. The candidates affirm the Scriptures and the Apostles' Creed. Former Roman priests renounce past errors and all clergy make a promise of conformity. The officiant (a bishop or a priest appointed by the bishop) gives absolution and formally receives the candidate by taking his or her right hand. Persons are not received through confirmation, but those who have not been confirmed are urged to seek it (although nothing defines who has or has not received confirmation). There is little to indicate how widely this form was used or for how long. It clearly represents another era.[2]

When, in the nineteenth century, the distinction in the manner of welcoming Protestants and Catholics became common in the

Episcopal Church, it was never embodied in rubrics or canons, and it seems never to have been given scholarly explanation and defense. Yet it became virtually universal in the Anglican churches that Catholics were received and Protestants confirmed.

A minor document that fills out the record is the 1949 edition of *The Book of Offices,* whose rites were not part of the Prayer Book but were approved by General Convention for use under the authorization of the diocesan bishop. This book contained a brief form to be used by the bishop "in admitting into the Communion of this Church persons already Confirmed in another part of the holy Catholic Church, not in communion with this Church." The bishops were already performing this pastoral action, but without any official text. Persons were presented to the bishop as "already confirmed." The recommended gesture was taking the candidate's right hand. The rubric did not expressly say that an "additional confirmation" was required of persons entering the Episcopal Church from some other churches.[3]

A 1969 canon of the Church of England says that baptized persons who are not episcopally confirmed must, on coming into the Church of England, be confirmed, while persons who have been episcopally confirmed "with unction or with the laying on of hands" shall be received.[4] This new canon simply codified the practice that had come to prevail.

III.

Some of the reasons that supported this distinction in the way persons were brought into the Episcopal Church from other Christian churches may be identified (or perhaps one should say surmised, since this distinction, whenever and however it was introduced, evidently stirred no comment or controversy). At the same time we may note some of the limitations in these reasons:

1. During the colonial period, the American churches had no bishops and hence no confirmations. When, in the early 1800s, the Episcopal Church came to have bishops who (on

the model of John Henry Hobart) undertook for the first time real pastoral oversight, many lifelong Episcopalians who had not received confirmation sought it. No doubt it seemed strange if persons from Protestant communions could come into membership without confirmation while adult Episcopalians were receiving it gratefully and in considerable numbers.

2. In those same years, the Episcopal Church sought to distinguish itself from "Protestant America." The sense of ecclesial identity that was implied in accepting the sacramental credentials of Catholics but not those of Protestants may trace to ideas such as the "branch theory" of catholicism argued by William Palmer, an associate of the Tractarians, in his work *The Church of Christ* (1838). However, both Palmer and the Tracts are generally silent on confirmation. Among some partisans, triumphalist claims were put forward implying that true ministry, sacraments, and even grace itself, inhere in a church's catholic substance, of which episcopacy is a necessary sign. Of course, such exclusive claims were vigorously denied by other Anglicans. The practice of receiving Catholics and confirming Protestants commended itself widely at about the time of this catholic initiative. Perhaps Episcopalians of all parties felt that it implied a welcome Anglican self-affirmation, while it did no one any harm.

3. Another influence may have been the "confirmation rubric": "And there shall none be admitted to the Holy Communion, until such time as he be confirmed, or be ready and desirous to be confirmed."[5] These words, literally read, placed persons from non-episcopal churches in much the same sacramental position as the church's own baptized but unconfirmed children, i.e., within the Christian community but ineligible for the Lord's Table.

This rubric traced to a thirteenth-century English regulation which sought to bring confirmation into more widespread use by making admission to communion clearly dependent on it. Beginning in 1549 this canon passed into Prayer Book rubrics. This rule originated as an internal discipline of medieval Christendom, a discipline which had no reference whatever to recognition among a plurality of baptizing Christian churches. Yet since the seventeenth century many persons must have thought that this Prayer Book rubric expressly forbade the admission to the Episcopal Church's table of baptized but unconfirmed members of other churches.

The qualification in the rubric allowing that readiness and desire for confirmation might suffice was added in the English revision of 1662 to cover persons who had been unable to receive confirmation during the years of Puritan rule. In the American Prayer Book, it also applied to the generations during which the church in the American colonies had had no bishops, and by necessity persons had been admitted to the Holy Communion without confirmation. The desire stood for the act. Indeed, for some years after the reorganization of the church in 1789, some dioceses and unorganized areas had no bishops, and access to confirmation was nearly as difficult as it had been during the colonial period. However, in time there were territorial dioceses from coast to coast, and ease of travel made episcopal visitation possible as never before. Yet this exception in the "confirmation rubric" remained unrevised after the conditions for which it was fully appropriate had passed.

Every rule is written with reference to a situation. To apply a law literally in a situation unlike that for which it was written may make it into a different rule. Yet this internal regulation of the late medieval English church was carried into a modern ecumenical situation quite different from that for which it was originally drawn up.

4. The Episcopal Church's understanding was no doubt influenced by the short lesson, Acts 8:14-17, which in the 1892 and 1928 Prayer Books was read at confirmation. This scripture reading tells of converts at Samaria who had been bap-

tized under the ministry of the "deacon," Philip, but did not receive the Holy Spirit until the apostles Peter and John came from Jerusalem and laid their hands on them. No doubt many Episcopalians thought that the passage described the practice of their own church: The local priest baptizes; but at a later time the bishop, representing the apostolic ministry, confers the Holy Spirit by the laying on of hands.

However, in the complex New Testament material, the sequence described in Acts 8 stands largely alone. John and Paul, the great theologians of the New Testament, think of conversion, forgiveness, church, baptism, and Spirit as a redemptive unity. The Roman Catholic exegete, Rudolph Schnackenburg, says: "One will seek in vain in the Pauline letters to discover a peculiar sacrament of the Spirit alongside baptism."[6] Only the Book of Acts describes a separate initiatory gift of the Holy Spirit, but it falls in different configurations. Sometimes evidence of the Holy Spirit precedes baptism rather than follows it (as at Pentecost, 2:1-41, and the Gentile Pentecost, 10:44-47). A giving of the Spirit occurs after baptism in only two places (in Samaria, 8:14-17; and at Ephesus, 19:1-7). Often Luke does not identify a Spirit-act at all; persons are simply "baptized" (16:15,33, among many instances).

The account of events in Samaria does not speak to the two-stage initiation that grew up in the West. It does not describe a visit by Peter and John to confirm all the fifth-graders, and it has no reference to what should be done to welcome baptized Christians who lack episcopal confirmation. It does not provide a model for sacramental practice; rather, it is set in the account of the church's developing mission. Could the church remain one, even as it spread geographically? Samaria was schismatic Jewish territory. The apostles came "from Jerusalem" (mentioned twice, Acts 8:14,25) to bind the new community of believers into the parent community. Reginald Fuller summarized:

> The separation of the laying on of hands in Acts 8 has nothing to do with the western medieval separation of

confirmation from baptism but is due rather to Luke's redactional interest in subordinating each successive new stage in the Christian mission to the Jerusalem church and its apostolate.[7]

The pattern in which conversion and baptism were followed by the sign of Spirit (the pattern of Samaria and Ephesus) was not continued in the initiatory practice of the second century. To make this text a New Testament precedent for initiatory rites which are the product of later western historical development stretches it beyond its limits.

5. Perhaps the Chicago-Lambeth Quadrilateral[8] had some influence. It was put forward in the late nineteenth century by Anglicans as a basis for the coming reunited church. One of its four proposals is that "the Historic Episcopate," locally adapted, is a constitutive factor in a reunited church. Some Anglicans may well have thought: According to the Lambeth statement, bishops are an integral part of the united church that is coming to be; we therefore hold the order in reverence against that time of reunion. Bishops, by ancient prerogative, confirm—their part in the church's initiatory act. We therefore recognize as fully initiate those members of other churches who have received episcopal confirmation, but we hold baptized persons who have not received episcopal confirmation to be without the initiatory ministration that signifies now the church that is to come.

Yet the carefully drafted Chicago-Lambeth Quadrilateral speaks of episcopacy without specifying that a bishop is necessarily the minister of an initiatory act called confirmation. It names the two sacraments of the Gospel, Baptism and the Supper of the Lord, making no mention that another rite might be required to complete the one or admit to the other. The Quadrilateral does not say that in our present dividedness, only episcopally ordered churches are truly and fully churches or that one can only become a complete Christian in a church which has bishops.

Historically, there have been bishops who presided at virtually all occasions of Christian initiation and were themselves the teachers of the newly baptized; there have been bishops who engaged in strenuous travel to visit and confirm; and there have been bishops on whom the burden of the church's initiatory rites rested very lightly. The role of bishops in the initiatory polity of a reunited church is surely one of the matters that might be "locally adapted."

If these were the more important evidences and arguments that supported past practice, they will not carry that weight today.

IV.

We may inquire about the actual role of bishops in Christian initiation in the churches whose members the Episcopal Church has by custom "received."

The Episcopal Church has unquestioningly "received" persons from Orthodox churches. The House of Bishops statement spoke of them as having already been confirmed, and the English canon cited above seems to have them in mind as persons who are episcopally confirmed "with unction." In the Eastern Orthodox churches, however, members are not confirmed by a bishop. Rather, infants a few days old are baptized and "chrismated" (i.e., anointed with chrism), and given the Holy Communion. Since the chrism is consecrated by the Patriarch or the bishop, some western observers have considered it a token presence of the bishop, thereby making eastern "chrismation" the equivalent of western "confirmation." Eastern Christians, however, usually see such an argument as an awkward attempt by Westerners to define them in western terms. In eastern thinking, it is simply the bishop's ministry to bless the chrism, and it is the priest's ministry to use the chrism blessed by the bishop. An Orthodox participant in a recent discussion remarked that if there is at baptism an extension of the bishop, it is not the blessed chrism but the priest.

If the Episcopal Church continues to "receive" persons from eastern churches, it should not do so on grounds that they have already been confirmed by a bishop. They have not.

To turn to the western tradition, the common initiatory pattern in the Roman communion is that persons baptized as infants will in later childhood (usually a few years after "first communion") be confirmed by a bishop. This divided initiatory rite of the West, in which baptism has been followed several years later by confirmation and first communion (or, in recent Roman practice, baptism, followed by first confession and first communion, then, in time, confirmation) has a history:

In the early church, baptism took place at the bishop's church at Easter. The water baptism in many (but not all) parts of the church was followed at once by an anointing (in some places by other post-baptismal acts as well), and the newly baptized were given communion. In time outlying congregations grew up, dependent on the bishop's church, but claiming more and more prerogatives for themselves. The right to baptize came to be exercised in such local congregations, the priest performing all parts of the ritual. (In other words, what is now done in the East was also done in most parts of the early medieval West.) However, in Rome and its vicinity, baptism was followed by two anointings: one by a presbyter, at the water, and evidently of the whole body; the second, shortly afterward, by the bishop, in the eucharistic room, and only of the forehead.

Reforms in the eighth century, seeking to bring liturgical order to early medieval Europe, introduced the rites of Rome throughout Charlemagne's realm. The practice of a second anointing by the bishop following baptism, a practice which had been exclusively Roman, became an expected part of initiatory ritual in regions that had not previously known it. However, in northern Europe dioceses were large, and travel difficult. One medieval law required that parents bring their children to the bishop when it became known that he was within seven miles. Such laws are made in desperation. The result was that the bishop's anointing was often simply not available, and when it could be had, it came several (often regularized at seven) years after a child had been baptized. In time, since the children who were confirmed were beginning to take some responsibility for themselves, a few rudimentary educational preconditions were added to confirmation, starting it on the way to becoming a sacrament of maturation. "Confirmation is to baptism as growth to birth."[9]

This late medieval rite in which two distinct ritual actions were linked to two distinct life-stages was inherited by the churches of the modern West, Catholic and Protestant. The largely accidental character of the process by which it had developed was not understood until relatively recently. The Roman church has regarded the sign in confirmation as anointing with chrism, while among Anglicans, Lutherans and others the sign has been the laying on of hands. Although the medieval church had not emphasized the taking on oneself the vows of baptism as part of confirmation, both the Reformation and Counter-Reformation stressed education, and since the sixteenth century, catechetical preparation for confirmation has received much emphasis throughout the West.

In recent generations, with ease of travel and many assisting bishops, Roman Catholics have, as a rule, been confirmed some years after their baptism, by bishops in the historic succession—but with a significant qualification:

Rome has traditionally understood that reserving the post-baptismal anointing to the bishop is a matter of discipline, rather than of divine ordinance. Although the bishop has been the ordinary minister of confirmation (as bishops had at one time been the ordinary ministers of the Eucharist), presbyters might, with authorization, be the extraordinary ministers of the rite.

This provision for confirmation by priests has been greatly extended in our own time. Following the Second Vatican Council (1962-65), the Sacred Congregation of Rites authorized a "Rite for the Christian Initiation of Adults"[10] which provides that prepared adults be baptized at the Easter Vigil, the baptism to be followed at once by confirmation and first communion. If a bishop is present, he confirms, although if the number of candidates is large, other clergy may share the action. If no bishop is present, the confirming is done entirely by presbyters. It is more important to keep the ritual unity of baptism, confirmation and eucharist than it is to preserve a distinct role for the bishop.

(The Roman rite for the baptism of children [1967] does anticipate that the baptized infants will later be confirmed by a bishop. However, some Roman liturgists are now asking why, if the unity of the initiatory actions is upheld in adult baptism, it should not be similarly observed in all baptisms.)

The result of this modern discipline is that many Roman Catholic priests confirm more or less regularly, and many lay persons (more as time goes along) are members in full standing, having been confirmed by a presbyter. Again, as in the case of persons from churches of the East, if the Episcopal Church wants to receive, rather than confirm, persons from the Roman church, it will have to do so on grounds other than that they have already been confirmed by a bishop. Many have not. Their church has not required it.

The Episcopal Church need not be protective. Catholicity does not require confirmation by bishops; the other churches which retain catholic substance either do not know or do not require it. Only Anglicanism has continued to associate bishops with this portion of initiatory ritual so rigorously. Is there danger that a practice which Anglicans have taken to be a mark of continuity and catholicity may come to seem an isolating Anglican idiosyncrasy?

V.

What of persons who come to the Episcopal Church from Protestant churches? Some of them have been confirmed in their former churches as young people, often after a serious preparatory regimen which enabled them to take upon themselves the responsibilities of baptism. Others, coming from the believer's baptism tradition, will have made a declaration of faith at the time of their baptism. Thus persons who come from Protestant communions and who are in full standing in those communions will have made, in ways appropriate to the traditions from which they come, mature witness to their faith and baptism. Yet the House of Bishops' statement of 1937 said they should receive "an additional confirmation at the hands of a bishop." No doubt such thinking took the previous confirmation to have been a pastoral action and an adequate rite of its own kind, although it lacked the sacramental dimension which confirmation in the Episcopal Church provided.

That House of Bishops' statement is more than half a century old, and the thinking behind it is not fully recoverable. The same body might conclude differently today. In any case, the issue by now needs to be readdressed. Several authoritative sources seem to question this requirement of "an additional confirmation":

1. Since 1979 the Prayer Book has said that "Holy Baptism is full initiation by water and the Holy Spirit into Christ's Body the Church,"[11] and the "confirmation rubric" has simply been dropped. The Canons second the Prayer Book, saying in Canon I.17.1(a) that all persons who have been baptized with water in the trinitarian name, "whether in this Church or in another Christian Church, and whose Baptisms have been duly recorded in this Church, are members thereof."

This understanding that baptism is one's full acceptance into Christ's church sharply questions the practice by which neither the church's own children nor adults coming from non-episcopal bodies have been admitted to full communicant status by reason of their baptism, but only by baptism plus episcopal confirmation.

2. The Chicago-Lambeth Quadrilateral identifies "the two sacraments, Baptism and the Supper of the Lord" among the divine, given factors in the spiritual constitution of the church.[12] What is begun in baptism is sustained in the Eucharist. To locate another rite in between which is thought to complete baptism and admit to the Holy Communion creates a step which confuses the sacramental economy which Anglicanism has proposed for the coming united church. The Lambeth statement finds no need to mention confirmation.

3. The ecumenically prepared statement *Baptism, Eucharist and Ministry (BEM),* which has been received with appreciation and respect, says:

> If baptism, as incorporation into the body of Christ, points by its very nature to the eucharistic sharing of Christ's body and blood, the question arises as to how a further and separate rite can be interposed between baptism and admission to communion.[13]

The Lambeth Quadrilateral and the *BEM* statement both address the problem: The one church of Christ exists only in its divided form. In the midst of this dividedness, what signs are there of oneness—oneness now and to come? These documents answer in part by citing baptism, which binds a believer not into a particular congregation or denomination, but into Christ and his people. This great mark of belonging should be given recognition among all Christian bodies, and that recognition should bring pressure to bear on resistant points of continuing non-recognition.

VI.

The considerations, Anglican and ecumenical, which have been cited here indicate significant consensus:

1. *the completeness and finality of baptism:* It is important to affirm that baptism is the effective sign of the Gospel, not of a portion of the Gospel. By it God is committed to us, and we to God. It conveys the central realities of faith: forgiveness, new birth, union with Christ, the gift of the Holy Spirit, full membership in the church, and eternal life. The relation between God and ourselves which is begun in baptism is enduring, for God is faithful, even when we are not. The engagement of the triune God with the totality of one of us is guaranteed, not by our experience, but by divine promise. Although this initiatory sign is given once, at the beginning of life in Christ and the church, and is not repeated, it stands for beginnings, for ends, and for all the way between.

2. *the necessity of being reminded of one's baptism:* Baptism is an
   act of promise, signifying all that is to follow. We do not grow
   beyond it, but into what it pledges. This fundamental sign of
   the divine self-investment in us does not become more distant
   with time. It is, in a sense, always present. Yet this objective
   sign, if it is to be creative in us, needs to be remembered,
   drawn on, repossessed.

In baptism, divine gift and promise are met by our faith and
commitment. Hooker spoke of the promises of baptism as "the
solemnest vow that we ever made."[14] Since we are forgetful, we
need to be reminded of the "Baptismal Covenant."[15] The vows of
baptism need to be confessed in new life situations.

The Prayer Book seeks to give ritual and pastoral form to these
understandings. It does so by saying all that can reverently and
properly be said for baptism as the foundational sign in us of eternal redemption. At the same time, it seeks to support the life of
faith that grows from baptism and reaches toward the eternal life
which baptism promises. (Liturgy might be thought of as a system
of prompts for our weak memories.) It does so by a full and adequate form for baptism, followed by occasions of reminding,
restatement and renewal.

VII.

Past Anglican Prayer Books sought to provide for the conscious,
intentional restating of one's baptismal commitment at one occasion: confirmation—ordinarily an adolescent rite of coming of age,
done once in a lifetime. Before looking at the provision of the
1979 Prayer Book for the renewal of the covenant of baptism, it
may be useful to look at this past single occasion of "ratifying and
confirming" the "solemn promise that...was made in your name at
your Baptism."[16]

A piece of analysis may be useful: Since the sixteenth century,
Prayer Book confirmation had brought together two distinguish-
able strands:

1. It continued the sacramental post-baptismal sign of the Spirit which had been part of the initiatory ritual of some (but not all) parts of the early church and which had been sustained as a bishop's ministry throughout the Middle Ages.

2. It was also the occasion for one's own renewal of the promises that had been made for one by others at one's baptism. This owning of the promises of baptism traced to catechetical emphases of Renaissance humanism, the Reformation, and the Counter-Reformation.

(The first strand was represented in the 1928 BCP by the bishop's prayer and laying on of hands, on the lower half of p.297; the second strand by the bishop's questions and the confirmands' answers, at the bottom of p.296 and the top of p.297.)

Although these two actions had been combined in Anglican confirmation (not always with perfect clarity) they were in character quite distinct. To set them in parallel:

The Seal of the Spirit	*Reaffirmation of the Promises of Baptism*
This is a sacramental rite, speaking of the Holy Spirit.	This is a catechetical rite, speaking of the renewal of baptismal promises.
Thus it is God's act; God is self-bestowed.	Thus it is a responsible human act.
The act is initiatory—part of becoming a Christian.	The act is within Christian life. One must be a Christian in order to have promises to reaffirm.
This act is unrepeatable, for it is a detached part of the unrepeated act of baptism.	This act is repeatable; indeed, it is often repeated.
It comes from the New Testament and the early church.	It comes from the medieval West, the Reformation and the Counter-Reformation.

These two clusters of meaning drew on different concepts and tended to move confirmation in different directions:

—Persons (generally liturgists and sacramental theologians) who thought in terms of the first cluster, the sign of the Spirit, referred to the Book of Acts, the early liturgies, and the theology of the Holy Spirit; and they proposed administering confirmation at an earlier age, closer to baptism.

—Other persons (generally Christian educators) who thought in terms of a catechetical observance, referred to developmental psychology—Piaget, Erikson, Gesel, Kohlberg, Gilligan—and the ways of learning. If confirmation signifies entry into adulthood, it should come later. Who is effectively adult at age twelve?

In the course of Prayer Book revision, it became clear that these two configurations of actions and meanings were not parts of a single thing. They were two different things, each with distinct origin and character, which had been united not because of their intrinsic oneness but by a series of historical accidents, and the combination had been given an after-the-fact theological rationale.

VIII.

It is hardly too much to say that the rite of confirmation was asked to do more than its history or theological rationale enabled it to do. Pastoral needs could be met best by some theological and ritual clarification.

The 1979 Prayer Book has divided the two acts that constituted past Anglican confirmation, allowing the specific character of each to be clearer:

1. *The sacramental, initiatory act, representing the objective divine seal of the Spirit,* is now set within the rite of baptism, where the prayer for the gifts of the Spirit and a laying on of hands (with optional anointing) immediately follow the water baptism. This act is to be done by the bishop if a bishop is present,[17] otherwise it is done by the officiating presbyter. The initiatory sequence culminates in the Eucharist.

Thus the Spirit-action of past confirmation is not dropped but is restored to the baptismal rite, the place from which it came and in which it is intelligible. (Prayer Books from 1552 to 1928 had in this post-baptismal location a reception of the newly baptized which used language of confessing the faith and engaging in combat for Christ—language from the pastoral side of the medieval understanding of confirmation. (Cranmer may have intended this language plus signing with the cross to represent presbyteral confirmation.) This action makes it clear that the Spirit is not an "extra," reserved for an elite within the baptized community—an elite created by instruction or by "riper years." The Spirit is given in baptism. God is a unity, and one cannot be brought into the divine family and under the sign of the cross and then encounter the Spirit several years later, when a second rite, administered by a distinct order of the ministry, makes up the deficiency in the first.

Some Anglican thought has associated the Holy Spirit with confirmation—sometimes to the diminishment of baptism. Yet Anglican liturgies and theologies have spoken of the agency of the Spirit in baptism. (The 1979 Prayer Book does so with unusual fullness.) Clearly a second initiatory giving of the Spirit is redundant. To deal with the theological problem of a divided initiatory ritual, some writers of a scholastic turn of mind have proposed that Christians meet the Spirit in one way at baptism, and in another way at confirmation. But persons meet persons as wholes; qualitative or quantitative distinctions are unsuited to describing the redemptive encounter with God.

In some churches the ritual words and actions of baptism are quite minimal, in others they are very elaborate. Yet any baptism, in any tradition, under any circumstances (including emergency circumstances), with water, using the triadic name, carried out in faith, and intending what the church intends, is a baptism—a divine act in which sins are forgiven, the Spirit is conferred, the people of Christ enclose a new life, and eternal life is pledged.

It is true that not all churches include in their baptismal words and acts an explicit sealing of the Spirit. Indeed, the Episcopal Church's rite did not include it until *Prayer Book Studies 18*, in 1970. The absence in any church's rite of a specific prayer for the gifts of the Spirit and an accompanying gesture of blessing does not compromise the trinitarian wholeness of its baptism—else the initiatory practice of the New Testament, along with much of the later church, is (or has been) gravely defective.

The Spirit-act which the Prayer Book now sets within the baptismal rite may be thought of as like the epiclesis—the explicit request for the agency of the Holy Spirit—which appears in many eucharistic prayers (including all of the eucharistic prayers of the American Prayer Book tradition). Some eucharistic texts, Roman and Anglican, have lacked an epiclesis. Yet that lack in the verbal action of the prayer did not keep the Holy Spirit away from the sacramental act or the eucharistic community, and it would be presumption to suppose that the Spirit is only present when that presence is prayed for. Yet, since the Spirit is present and active in the sacrament, it seems desirable that the liturgies say so. Similarly, the prayer for the Spirit and the action which follow baptism articulate an important aspect of the baptismal reality; they contribute to the fullness of the sign. They form part of the total initiatory statement. Rather than being placed later in time where they could seem to offer some gift over and above baptism, they stand within the initiatory act where they bring to explicitness a constitutive feature of Holy Baptism.

2. *As to the pastoral, catechetical rite whose substance is the renewal of the baptismal covenant,* this act is not initiatory and thus is not part of becoming Christian; rather, it stands within the pastoral economy of the church to undergird, as needed, a baptized person's custody of life.

In a sense, each Eucharist and each absolution is a restatement and renewal of one's baptism, but they are so implicitly. Expressly, the baptismal promises are spoken anew by the community at several occasions: at each baptism, at the Easter Vigil, and they may be used at the specified baptismal occasions even when there is no baptism.[18]

Yet these fundamental promises can also be restated on occasions that support and interpret an individual Christian's later experience. The Prayer Book identifies three such occasions: Confirmation, Reception, and Reaffirmation, of which more must be said.

IX.

Confirmation: The Prayer Book describes confirmation specifically as the first occasion of adult restatement of baptismal commitments by one who had been baptized in infancy. At confirmation one affirms for oneself the promises that were made in one's name by others at baptism. It is expressly intended for "those who are baptized at an early age" and who later take occasion to "make a mature public affirmation"; it is a waymark as one of the church's own children grows into conscious, internalized faith.[19] It is, so to speak, a pastoral and catechetical complement of infant baptism. This rite (as stipulated in a statement jointly issued in 1972 by the Theological and Prayer Book Committees of the House of Bishops and the Standing Liturgical Commission) is not a "completion of baptism" nor a condition for admission to the Holy Communion.[20] At a chosen life-moment a maturing baptized person affirms publicly for her or himself the pledges of baptism and is met by the bishop's prayer and blessing. This being its function, "confirmation" is not suitable for committed and active adult Christians who come to the Episcopal Church from another.[21]

Reaffirmation: Renewing one's baptismal vows is a repeatable act and may be used for a variety of personal occasions at any stage of adulthood. A report of the 1991 International Anglican Liturgical Consultation says that "There is no limit to the number of times the baptismal promises may be affirmed."[22] At moments of restoration or of fresh beginning, baptized Christians may repossess their fundamental starting place in Christ and the church by reaffirming the promises of their baptism; and they ask for the further strengthening of the Spirit.

Such a public adult restatement of the Christian vows may be made by any baptized person, as appropriate to his or her individual biography in faith; such later occasions are called "reaffirmation." With this Prayer Book provision in place, pastoral wisdom is discovering how it may function to interpret the varied and often discontinuous experiences of Christians in the late twentieth century.

Reception: As the Prayer Book makes provision for renewing one's baptismal promises at "confirmation" and "reaffirmation," it also speaks of "reception."

In our individualistic, mobile society, the chosen factors in life increase in importance, while the given factors reduce. Many persons pass—thoughtfully, rather than casually—from one religious affiliation to another. Yet baptism, which has its origins in the apostolic life which antedates all our present-day divisions, is a deep sign of oneness among the diverse Christian communions. The way in which the objective completeness of baptism is treated in cases of persons who are received from other churches is a test of the Episcopal Church's belief in the "one baptism" which it professes in the Nicene Creed.[23] Christ is not divided, and baptism unites persons to the one Christ. Recognizing the wholeness and totality which by divine gift inhere in baptism, the Episcopal Church should not seem to say to baptized Christians from non-episcopal bodies, "Something essential to your relation to God and the church was lacking (except perhaps in some uncovenanted way) in what you had before. We here confer it." Demonstrably, empirically, the signs of the Spirit (i.e., love, joy, peace, patience, kindness, Christian courage) are at least as evident in churches which lack episcopal confirmation as they are in churches which have it. Such empirical observation carries theological significance.

Probably few Episcopalians would be at ease today with the sacramental exclusiveness that had long been common. J.A.T.

Robinson forty years ago expressed his discomfort over a distinction he questioned but felt himself required to maintain:

> When a person is admitted to Anglicanism from the Roman Communion there is a formal act of reception. Ought not such a service to be held in other cases as well—so as to let Confirmation. . . stand out for what it is, part of the Catholic wholeness of Christian initiation, and not something made necessary by our unhappy divisions? The *disciplinary* use of Confirmation, in relation to those outside Anglicanism, is a modern phenomenon and one much to be regretted. When Confirmation is allowed to become a sort of tariff wall in interdenominational trade discussions, I as an Anglican find myself shamed and embarrassed.[24]

The Prayer Book speaks of confirmation as an in-the-family observance for those who had been baptized "at an early age," but never as an action which defines divisions among churches. Although confirmation so described is inappropriate for adult newcomers to the Episcopal Church, there is reason for asking baptized adults, as they enter a new faith community, to recognize freshly the promises of God to themselves and to reaffirm their own promises to God—promises which are constitutive of their very identity as Christians. Since one is coming to an episcopally-ordered church, a bishop, representing the worldwide, centuries-old people of God, recognizes one's fundamental status as a baptized person, and, by name and with prayer, receives one on renewal of the common baptismal pledges.

The report of the 1991 International Anglican Liturgical Consultation, referred to above, concludes that at the point of reception, the distinction "between those already confirmed or sealed in a Christian tradition which has retained the historic episcopate, and members of other Communions...is no longer appropriate." However, it commends an act of reception and welcome by the bishop.[25]

X.

The 1979 revision of the Prayer Book changed the initiatory polity of the Episcopal Church in ways that made necessary a new canonical definition of membership. What becomes of those little boxes "B," "C," and "C" (*B*aptized, *C*onfirmed, *C*ommunicant) in parish records now that persons, including small children, are admitted to communion by reason of their baptism, and now that it is not required that all adults, to be in good standing, have been episcopally confirmed? The General Conventions of 1982 and 1985 adopted Canon I.17 on membership.

Canon 17 begins (I.17.1[a]) by indicating that all membership roots in baptism and that recognized baptism may be received in any Christian church:

> All persons who have received the Sacrament of Holy Baptism with water in the Name of the Father, and of the Son, and of the Holy Spirit, whether in this Church or in another Christian Church, and whose Baptisms have been duly recorded in this Church, are members thereof.

The term "duly recorded" is obviously important. The canon takes for granted that persons who are baptized in the Episcopal Church as infants are members, "duly recorded." When they become sixteen years of age, they are considered adult members (b).

Sub-sections (c) and (d) speak of adult members. Sub-section (c), following the second rubric on p.412 of the Prayer Book, says that "it is expected" that adult members will affirm the responsibilities of their baptism before the bishop in confirmation or reception. This wording assumes that the persons presented for confirmation or reception are already adult members of the church. In a sense, the local congregation is the primary agent of reception. A person has already been brought into the church's life of faith, worship and service before she or he is presented to the bishop. The bishop's role is performative, but performative in the way in which acts of recognition or ratification are performative. One is made a member in the fundamental act of God in the church: baptism. Confirmation and reception are ways in which the church guides and supports decisive moments in the lives of persons who are already adult members.

Sub-section (d) clarifies that *for the purposes of this and all other canons,* a person shall be considered *as both baptized and confirmed*

> *— who is baptized in this Church as an adult and receives the laying on of hands by the Bishop at Baptism*

Comment: Adults who are baptized when a bishop is present and ministers the post-baptismal prayer and action (as the third rubric on p.298 of the BCP expects) are fully initiate. A "mature public affirmation" of faith is part of the baptism itself, and the seal of the Spirit, which includes the bishop's gesture of bonding and blessing, takes place within the baptismal action. The initiatory passage is in all respects complete. Any repetition of any part of this initiatory action is redundant, and being redundant, trivializes the Prayer Book liturgy of initiation. Baptism of an adult with a bishop presiding is the pastoral situation for which the Prayer Book rite of Holy Baptism functions with greatest clarity and economy.

> *—who is baptized in this Church as an adult and at some time after Baptism receives the laying on of hands by the Bishop in Reaffirmation of Baptismal Vows*

Comment: Adults who are baptized by a presbyter (or by any other minister, not a bishop) are at once admitted to the Holy Communion. When subsequently they are presented to a bishop (which the second rubric on p.412 of the BCP as well as Canon I.17.1(c) say is "expected") *they are not then confirmed;* rather, they *reaffirm* their promises—promises which they made with full awareness at the time of their baptism. The bishop lays hands on them and prays for them by name (BCP, pp.310 and 419). The act is a welcome and a support for the baptized person and an expression of the pastoral role of the bishop.

—who received the laying on of hands at Confirmation (by any Bishop in apostolic succession) and is received into the Episcopal Church by a Bishop of this Church
    Comment: This provision sustains past custom. Confirmation in another episcopally-ordered church is not repeated; it is recognized, and the adult is received.

—who received the laying on of hands by a Bishop of this Church at Confirmation or Reception.
    Comment: Either confirmation or reception by a bishop of the Episcopal Church establishes one as a baptized and confirmed member.

Confirmation, reception, and reaffirmation are functionally and pastorally different, but the thrust of this canon is that for purposes of determining "confirmed" membership, these three actions, carried out by the bishop's prayer and laying on of hands, are regarded as equivalent. To put it from the point of view of the member, all adult Episcopalians are "expected" to have been presented to a bishop, at one stage of life or another, as their individual circumstances direct, for the laying-on of hands—a gesture of bonding and blessing. They will not all have been "confirmed." To put it from the point of view of the bishop, the bishop does not confirm all, but (as befits an episcopally-ordered community) the bishop does have a pastoral role in bringing persons into the church's membership and maintaining them in their life in the community of faith.

XI.

The sum of this argument is that no distinction should be made between baptized Christians of mature faith who come to the

Episcopal Church from other communions. Such persons are all fully initiate sacramentally, and they are all at this occasion doing the same thing, viz., promising to carry out the obligations of their baptism in the responsibilities and satisfactions of the Episcopalian community of faith. If the distinction between receiving Catholics and confirming Protestants is not required as a matter of principle, in our ecumenical era it should be a matter of principle to see that it is discontinued.

The pastoral administration of passage into the Episcopal Church involves more than rubrics and canons. In a matter as personal and varied as bringing baptized persons from a former affiliation, Catholic or Protestant, into a Christian community in the Anglican obedience, there is need for pastoral judgment. (Although the 1979 Prayer Book heightens the need for such judgment, it does not introduce the factor for the first time.) Yet there are few express criteria to guide those who must make such judgments. How shall "mature faith" be determined? Persons who were baptized in another church but who later received no nurture whatever in Christian faith and life should no doubt be confirmed. Their discovery of the Episcopal Church is at the same time their discovery of Christian faith. But what of those who received some prior instruction, but not very much? And of course there are many who come to the Episcopal Church from other traditions after a period of search and intelligent inquiry. They may welcome some ordered introduction to the history, the beliefs and the (perhaps somewhat puzzling) ways of the church to which they have been attracted. However, such preparation for informed membership does not reflect on the adequacy of their sacramental credentials. Indeed, their coming into a new faith community will usually be an occasion for mutual giving and receiving in the life of the Spirit. Among the baptized, all is exchange.

Pastoral issues with regard to children will arise, perhaps in some new ways. The rubrics and canons assume only the reception into the Episcopal Church of responsible, competent adults. However, such adults will often be parents of small children, and the Episcopal Church's welcome of baptized persons must extend to those children. The theology that lets adults speak for children at baptism—a theology usually based on the unity of the household and the interconnectedness of persons in Christ—may be extended. A parental decision to live the responsibilities of baptism in a new faith community may carry the children as well. Children too young to speak or decide for themselves should be included in the reception of their parents. As with adults, everything that is done in connection with the incorporation of such children into the life of the Episcopal Church should affirm and recognize their prior standing as baptized Christians. They should be registered as baptized, communicating members, and in ways appropriate to their age they begin at once to take their part in the church's life of word and sacrament, learning, caring, and mission.

Perhaps one must ask specifically: Should children who were received by a bishop, perhaps at quite a young age, later come to confirmation? To venture an answer: Confirmation is a pastoral rite on which no sacramental privilege depends. It is, however, "expected." Thus confirmation should not be regimented by age or grade in school, but should be voluntary—a sign of one's growing awareness in matters of faith and church responsibilities. This opportunity to declare oneself as one comes of age in the church should be as open to persons who had been received in early childhood by a bishop as to any other child in the church.

Parish clergy must be prepared to make pastoral judgments and to explain them to the persons involved, to the congregation, and to the bishop. There is little model for such discrimination; yet the matter is important, and experience can be gained quite quickly— unless the pastoral issues go unaddressed.

XII.

The initiatory rites of the 1979 Prayer Book have been in use now for a decade and a half, and the present canon on membership in effect for almost as long. In recent years there has been much ecumenical awareness of the foundational place of baptism in the life of the church and of the individual Christian. To some extent, the logic of these factors has been making its own case, and in parts of the Episcopal Church the distinction between receiving some baptized Christians and confirming others is ending or is under question.

Some guidelines issued by the Diocese of Connecticut in 1990 say with respect to "reception":

> Persons presented for Reception are those who have been baptized with water in the Name of the Trinity, have previously made a mature public affirmation of faith in any other Christian communion (either at their Baptism or on a separate occasion), and now desire to live their faith within the fellowship of the Episcopal Church. Thus, the same rite of Reception is applicable without distinction to, for example, a Southern Baptist who was baptized at age 12, a Roman Catholic baptized in infancy and confirmed in early adolescence by a bishop (or a priest acting for a bishop), and a Lutheran baptized in infancy and confirmed as an adolescent by the parish pastor. The criterion distinguishing candidates for Reception from those for Confirmation is their own maturity at the time they made public avowal of faith, rather than the apostolicity of the minister who presided on that occasion.[26]

The publication of these Connecticut guidelines in *Open* indicates the concurrence of Associated Parishes and the national Association of Diocesan Liturgy and Music Commissions. Some jurisdictions—among them Chicago, Maryland, Indianapolis, Central New York, New Hampshire, Western North Carolina, Michigan, Western Michigan and Northern Michigan—have begun to "receive" all persons who were baptized and have come to full membership in another church. An advisory committee of the Diocese of Washington reported along similar lines. Other dioceses have their policies under discussion.

In his essay, "Rites of Initiation," Charles Price spoke to this matter:

If adults baptized in another church have already made a mature commitment to Christ in their former denomination, *they should be received by the bishop.* The appropriate manual act for the reception of new members from any denomination—whether Roman Catholic, Orthodox, Lutheran, or Baptist—is the laying on of hands, to symbolize that special link to the whole church which our bishops represent to us. Such adults also receive strengthening power of the Spirit through prayer and the laying on of hands. The appropriate formula is that for reception.[27]

Comment: The expectation of "mature commitment" must not be taken so literally as to question persons from Eastern churches, whose liturgical system has no public occasion of owning the faith comparable to Protestant or Catholic confirmation or to baptism of adults "on profession of faith" in the believer's baptism tradition. Presumably a life of adult faithfulness speaks for them.

Perhaps widely accepted customs which are as old as living memory will only change slowly. Yet differences among episcopal jurisdictions in this matter are not desirable. Insofar as canons and charters make certain rights or eligibilities in the church contingent upon adequate membership credentials, differences within a national church in so basic a matter as membership can produce sacramental and canonical injustice. Moreover, the practice of receiving Catholics and confirming Protestants constitutes an ecumenical awkwardness at best or offense at worst, and the ecclesiology it implies encourages Anglican self-delusion.

XIII.

Have dioceses which now receive persons from all Christian communions and dioceses which continue the old distinctions both thought the matter through and simply come out at different places? Or are some dioceses continuing past practice unexamined? Must this issue be addressed by each diocese independently?

It is important that the matter be under discussion—among bishops, national and diocesan commissions, parish clergy, and congregations. The issues are theological, ecumenical, liturgical, and pastoral. Discussion should take its rise from a theology of the gospel and the church, from informed ecumenical understanding, and from the Episcopal Church's official formularies.

This paper, written in aid of such discussion, proposes that the Prayer Book initiatory rites and the canon on membership, as they now stand, make it possible for the church to act with integrity and generosity in a matter in which past practice has become indefensible.

NOTES

1. "The House of Bishops Begins Discussions," in *The Living Church*, Oct. 6, 1937, p. 476.

2. Edward C. Cardwell, *Synodalia: A Collection of Articles of Religion, Canons, and Proceedings of Convocations in the Province of Canterbury from the Year 1547 to the Year 1717*, Vol. II (Oxford: Oxford University Press, 1842), pp. 796-804. My attention was called to this document by Prof. Marion Hatchett.

3. *The Book of Offices: Services for Certain Occasions not provided for in the Book of Common Prayer*, 2nd ed. (New York: Church Pension Fund, 1949), pp. 1-2.

4. 1969 Canons of the Church of England, B.28.

5. BCP 1928, p. 299.

6. *Baptism in the Thought of St. Paul*, trans. G. R. Beasley-Murray (New York: Herder and Herder, 1964), p. 91.

7. "Christian Initiation in the New Testament," in *Made, Not Born: New Perspectives on Christian Initiation and the*

Catechumenate (Notre Dame, IN: University of Notre Dame Press, 1976), p. 14.

8. BCP 1979, pp. 876-78.

9. Thomas Aquinas, *Summa Theologica* III, q. 72, art. 6.

10. RCIA, first English edition, 1974; revised ed., 1988.

11. BCP 1979, p. 298.

12. Ibid., pp. 876-78.

13. "Baptism," in *Baptism, Eucharist and Ministry,* Faith and Order Paper No. 111 (Geneva: World Council of Churches, 1982), commentary on par. 14.

14. Richard Hooker, *Of the Laws of Ecclesiastical Polity* (1594, 1597, 1600) V.lxv.9.

15. BCP 1979, pp. 304-305.

16. "The Order of Confirmation," in BCP 1928, p. 296.

17. BCP 1979, p. 298, third rubric.

18. Ibid., pp. 304-305, 292-294, 312.

19. Ibid., pp. 412, 860.

20. "Statement of Agreed Positions," in *Holy Baptism, together with A Form for Confirmation or the Laying-On of Hands by the Bishop with the Affirmation of Baptismal Vows,* Prayer Book Studies 26 (New York: Church Hymnal, 1973), pp. 3-4.

21. See below, p. 79.

22. "Walk in Newness of Life: The Findings of the International Anglican Liturgical Consultation, Toronto 1991," in *Growing in Newness of Life,* ed. David Holeton (Toronto, Canada: Anglican Book Centre, 1993), sec. 3, par. 20.

23. BCP 1979, pp. 328, 359.

24. "Our Present Position in the Light of the Bible," in *Becoming a Christian: Report of the Parish and People Conference 1953 on Baptism and Confirmation,* ed. Basil Minchin (New York: Morehouse-Gorham, 1954), p. 55.

25. "Walk in Newness of Life," sec. 3, par. 22.

26. The Episcopal Diocese of Connecticut, "Revised Diocesan Guidelines on Christian Initiation 1990," *Open* (Winter, 1990), pp. 3-8.

27. See below, p. 96.

Appendix

Rites of Initiation

The Reverend Charles P. Price
September 1984

The purpose of this paper is to clarify as much as possible some of the confusion surrounding the rites of initiation in the 1979 Book of Common Prayer. In particular it will examine the relation of Baptism to Confirmation and the rites for the reception of new members and the reaffirmation of baptismal vows. Certain practices will be recommended to secure consistency of administration throughout the church.

I.

1. The initiatory rite in BCP 1979 is the service of Holy Baptism. That rite comprises the following elements:

- Proclamation of the Word of God.
- Presentation and Examination of the Candidates.
- The Baptismal Covenant (basically the Creed).
- Thanksgiving over Water.
- Consecration of Chrism. (This element of the service is used only by the bishop.)
- The Baptism.

—Each candidate is presented by name.
—The celebrant or an assisting priest or deacon immerses each candidate or pours water on each one.

—The celebrant prays over the candidates, using a form of the prayer for the seven-fold gifts of the Spirit.

—The bishop or priest places a hand on the person's head, marking the forehead with a sign of the cross, using chrism if desired.

—The newly baptized are welcomed.

—The Peace is exchanged.

- The Eucharist may follow, although an alternative ending is provided. It must be recognized that circumstances may arise when the celebration of the Eucharist is impossible. Nevertheless, the Eucharist was anciently the climax and conclusion of the initiatory rite, and should be so regarded in BCP 1979.[1]

The service so outlined is the complete rite of initiation. Nothing else is *required* for full membership in the church. The "confirmation rubric" of earlier English and American books, which stipulated that no one could be admitted to Holy Communion unless confirmed or "ready and desirous of being confirmed," has been dropped.[2]

2. In other words, Confirmation as it appears in BCP 1979 is not a prerequisite to communion. Baptized infants may receive the Eucharist. The recent experience of the church with infant communion makes it increasingly clear that every argument against infant communion also counts against infant baptism. ("They aren't old enough to know what they're doing.") Conversely, all the arguments for infant baptism apply to the admission of the youngest children to the Lord's Table. ("Even the youngest are part of God's family.") The admission of young children to communion is a pastoral matter, to be worked out between parents and parish priest.[3] Basically it ought to be encouraged.

II.

3. Little is known about the earliest baptismal liturgies. References in Acts[4] (ca. 75 C.E.), *Didache*[5] (ca. 100 C.E.), and Justin Martyr[6] (ca. 150 C.E.) seem to imply that baptism involved only water, probably poured over the candidates' heads, either "in the name of the Lord Jesus Christ" or "in the name of the Father, and of the Son, and of the Holy Spirit."[7] Protestant churches have returned to the New Testament for as much of their practice as possible. They insist that water-baptism alone is essential for full membership in the church. It seems difficult to contest that position by appeal to a scriptural norm.

4. The first text known to us of a full baptismal liturgy comes from the *Apostolic Tradition,* attributed to Hippolytus, a document of the early third century.[8] It is quite an elaborate service. It provides for thanksgiving over oil of thanksgiving, exorcism of oil of exorcism, renunciation of "Satan, and all thy servants, and all thy works," anointing with oil of exorcism by a presbyter, affirmation of a creed remarkably similar to the Apostles' Creed during baptism in water, and anointing with oil of thanksgiving by a presbyter after the baptism. At the end, the bishop lays a hand on each of the candidates, anoints them again with oil of thanksgiving and signs them with a cross on the forehead. Most of these elements have been taken into the liturgy for baptism in the BCP 1979.

5. Although the service in *Apostolic Tradition* is considerably more elaborate than the liturgy which can reasonably be inferred to lie behind the description in Acts, *Didache,* and Justin, the added elements contribute no new meaning. They emphasize and dramatize what is implied in water-baptism: the gift of the Holy Spirit,[9] membership in the royal priesthood of Christ,[10] and bearing his cross.[11] They do not add anything essentially new. Otherwise, the completeness of earlier baptisms would be called into question, and the Lord's institution of baptism itself might be deemed incomplete.[12]

6. In Eastern Orthodoxy a rite with elements analogous to everything found in *Apostolic Tradition*—and more besides—persists to this day.[13] Presbyters, however, have been authorized to perform the whole service, including the last part, reserved in *Apostolic Tradition* for the bishop. In Rome, on the other hand, and eventually throughout the western Catholic Church, presbyters were authorized to preside at the first part of the service but bishops retained control over the final ceremonies: laying on of a hand, chrismation, and consignation.[14] This last part of the service, which became separated in place and time from the first, was called, variously, *perfection* or *completion,* or *confirmation.*[15] After some time, it came to be regarded as a separate sacrament,[16] although the close connection with baptism always remained. While one could receive communion without confirmation if in danger of death, and while such a person died in the communion of the church, nevertheless that person's baptism was in some sense incomplete. One was expected to be "confirmed" or "completed" as soon as possible after baptism.[17]

7. Thus baptism without confirmation was an ambiguous act. Was it or was it not complete? And confirmation without baptism became, as someone has said, a rite in search of a theology. Did it confer the Holy Spirit in a different way? Or did it represent, as came to be thought later, a rite of passage to maturity? All of these? In fact, possibly because of this lack of clarity, confirmation tended to fall into neglect during the Middle Ages. Even the best efforts of various local synods failed to enforce its use.[18] The "confirmation rubric" of earlier Anglican Prayer Books was devised in 1281, as is well-known, *to encourage confirmation, not to exclude from communion.*[19] Nothing short of this threatened excommunication had served that purpose; and, as things worked out, not even this drastic measure succeeded in bringing children to an early completion of their baptisms. Later medieval practice consequently tended to postpone confirmation until "years of discretion." Thomas Aquinas understood confirmation as a "sacrament of maturity," bringing an increase of grace for a different phase of life.[20] Yet even he argued that confirmation could be received by infants through the representation of their sponsors. When a bishop was present, baptism, confirmation,

and communion continued to be administered to infants, in the ancient manner. Bishop Stokesly of London baptized Elizabeth Tudor when she was three days old, and Archbishop Cranmer confirmed her immediately afterward.[21]

8. Nevertheless, confirmation came more and more to be postponed, and the interval used for instruction. Baptism, first communion, and confirmation were all separated by appreciable intervals of time, though different arrangements prevailed in different parts of the world. In some regions (notably in Spain and hence parts of Latin America), confirmation still occurs immediately after baptism; but elsewhere it is usually postponed until the fourth or seventh year. The catechism of the Council of Trent speaks of "the age of reason."[22] On the Continent, first communion usually precedes confirmation.

After the Reformation, the Church of England accepted the late medieval fragmentation, with first communion coming after confirmation "at years of discretion," in accordance with the Sarum rubric of 1281. The term "years of discretion" has never been officially defined.

III.

9. In view of the fact that both the practice and meaning of confirmation had become so hard to define, the first plan of the framers of the 1979 initiatory rite was to restore baptism to its ancient integrity and to eliminate confirmation as a separate service, on the Eastern Orthodox model. Such a rite was proposed in *Prayer Book Studies 18* (1970) and in *Services for Trial Use* (1970), where Holy Baptism appears much as it does in BCP 1979 under the title *Holy Baptism with the Laying-on-of-Hands*.

10. The parts of the service following water-baptism in all three of these texts are *like* the confirmation service of earlier Anglican books, in that they begin with the prayer for the seven-fold gifts of the Spirit. Some form of this prayer has appeared in the

Confirmation service of English and American Prayer Books since 1549 and in medieval Latin confirmation rites at least since the time of the Gelasian sacramentary, a document from the eighth century.[23] They also involve the laying of the celebrant's hands on the candidate. The use of oil, signing with the sign of the cross, and the formula of sealing with the Holy Spirit are part of the traditional pre-Reformation rite of confirmation. They are signs of the restored unity of the rite.

11. However, the parts of the service following water-baptism in these texts are *unlike* the older confirmation service, in that the minister of them may be a presbyter. As we have seen, in Eastern Orthodox churches, presbyters have been the appointed ministers of the whole rite of baptism, including this part, from a very early time.

12. PBS 18 proved unacceptable. Although the confirmation service of earlier Anglican Prayer Books, with some changes, had been restored to the liturgy for baptism, the new rite of initiation made no provision for commitment to Christ at the years of discretion. *For purposes of discussion we shall call the older confirmation service Confirmation A.* When Confirmation A became once more part of baptism, there was no opportunity for persons baptized as infants to confess their faith in Christ as they reached an age of maturity and as faith developed, or to receive the strengthening of the Spirit at such a crucial time. To meet this need, *A Form of Commitment to Christian Service* was first proposed.[24]

13. Further discussion revealed that even this provision was not sufficient to meet the felt need. A service of public commitment and empowerment was called for, involving the participation of the bishop, as the representative, in Episcopal polity, of the whole church. Consequently, a more formal rite for mature commitment was proposed in 1973, including affirmation of baptismal vows and laying on of hands by the bishop. This new service was, by popular demand, called *Confirmation,* despite the possibility of misunderstanding. *For purposes of this discussion we shall call Confirmation as it appeared in 1973 and in BCP 1979 Confirmation B.*

14. Confirmation B is *like* confirmation in earlier Anglican Prayer Books, chiefly in that its minister must be a bishop. It also involves laying on of hands. The formula, "Defend, O Lord, this thy child..." associated with confirmation since 1552, may still be used, although an alternative formula is provided.

15. On the other hand, Confirmation B is *unlike* confirmation in earlier Anglican books in that it no longer includes the traditional prayer for the seven-fold gifts of the Spirit; and the laying on of hands, rather than the laying on of *a hand,* is directed.[25] The formula, "you are sealed by the Holy Spirit in Baptism..." echoes the Orthodox formula for chrismation at the end of baptism: "The seal of the gift of the Holy Spirit." Therefore, *it is the last portion of Baptism which more closely resembles confirmation in earlier Anglican Prayer Books* (Confirmation A).

The use of the title *Confirmation* to apply to *Confirmation B* is the chief source of ambiguity about the present initiatory rite.

16. As BCP 1979 took shape, the revisers realized the need for two other liturgical provisions, not covered in earlier English or American books: (1) for the reception of new members already baptized in other denominations and (2) for the reaffirmation of baptismal vows on the part of Episcopalians whose faith had undergone a significant deepening since confirmation. As in confirmation itself (Confirmation B), the appropriate action on the part of the candidates at such critical turning points in their lives is a reaffirmation of baptismal vows, and the appropriate action on the part of the church is a prayer for the renewing power of the Spirit, accompanied by some symbolic gesture on the part of the bishop in the name of the whole church.

Therefore, these services were combined under the title *Confirmation, with forms for Reception and for the Reaffirmation of Baptismal Vows* (BCP 1979, pp. 412-419). This material is also included within the service of Holy Baptism as a convenience, because it is likely to be used with Baptism at the bishop's visit. However, strictly speaking, Confirmation (Confirmation B), Reception, and Reaffirmation are not parts of Holy Baptism. Confirmation A *is* part of Holy Baptism.

17. The result of the evolution described in paragraphs 9-16 is an initiatory rite capable of at least two interpretations.

> (a) Many Episcopalians, including a number of bishops, recognize no substantial change in the initiatory rites. As it always did, Christian initiation in BCP 1979 consists of Holy Baptism, Confirmation (here referred to as Confirmation B), and first communion. These elements appear in BCP 1979 as they have in every earlier English and American BCP. It is true that baptized persons may now be admitted to communion without confirmation; but confirmation is still the "expected" completion of baptism. The similarities between Confirmation B and the earlier rite of confirmation have been noted.
>
> The elements which follow water-baptism in BCP 1979, this argument runs, are really no substitute for confirmation unless done by a bishop. If a presbyter baptizes, Confirmation B is required to complete baptism.
>
> Those who interpret the provision of BCP 1979 in this way will expect confirmation to be administered *not only to "those baptized at an early age,"* but also to those baptized in other denominations who have not received episcopal laying on of hands, as well as those baptized in this church as adults by presbyters.
>
> By this interpretation, those who have received laying on of hands by a bishop (in apostolic succession) in another denomination will be *received,* as before, usually with a handshake. Those who, having been con-

firmed, elect to reaffirm their baptismal vows will be acknowledged, *but not with laying on of hands.* No manual acts, it will be noted, are prescribed for Reception and Reaffirmation (BCP 1979, pp. 418-419).

In all this there is no change in practices heretofore virtually universal in the Episcopal Church. *This interpretation of BCP 1979 is possible, but it is not the one intended by those who prepared the rite.*

(b) Those who accept the intention of the revisers acknowledge that this liturgy for Holy Baptism 1979 has restored the primitive unity of baptism, confirmation, and first communion. The addition of the prayer for the seven-fold gifts of the Spirit, the provision for anointing (though optional), and the formula, "N., you are sealed by the Holy Spirit..." are the hallmarks of ancient confirmation. Confirmation A is the ancient sacrament, now placed in conjunction with water baptism, as it was anciently. Holy Baptism in BCP 1979 has again become the full and complete service which it was in *Apostolic Tradition,* and which it still is in Eastern Orthodox churches, where presbyters are the designated ministers of the entire rite. In BCP 1979, the celebrant is the bishop when present; "In the absence of a bishop, a priest is the celebrant and presides" at the whole service.

18. Those who interpret BCP 1979 in this latter way will treat Confirmation, Reception, and Reaffirmation as follows:

(a) All those baptized at an early age, even with the reassembled liturgy, are expected to be confirmed (Confirmation B) by the bishop. *Confirmation B is the rite of maturity needed when baptism and Confirmation A have been reunited.* Confirmation B should be administered at a later rather than at an earlier age. Admission to communion no longer depends on it. It must be undertaken willingly and deliberately.

(b) *Adults baptized in the Episcopal Church should not be "confirmed."* For adults, baptism, which includes Confirmation A, is a mature profession of faith, an act complete in itself.

(i) Adults baptized by a presbyter should publicly *reaffirm their baptismal vows* before the bishop, and receive laying on of hands in order to establish symbolically their tie to the whole church. The appropriate prayer is the one for Reaffirmation of Baptismal Vows. That is to say, the rubric which requires adults baptized by a presbyter to receive laying on of hands (BCP 1979, p. 412) may be complied with by using *laying on of hands as the bishop's manual act for Reaffirmation.*[26] As noted previously, no manual act is specified.[27]

(ii) Adults baptized with the laying on of a hand by a bishop (Confirmation A) require no further liturgical act.[28]

(c) Adults baptized in other churches who wish to become members of this church do so canonically by having their baptisms duly recorded in this church.[29] We acknowledge baptism in water in the name of the Trinity as the sole requirement for membership in this Christian community. (See para. 3.)

(d) It must then be ascertained in pastoral conversation with such adults whether they have made a mature commitment to Christ. If they have not, and if they have been baptized in infancy, they are expected to be confirmed by the bishop (Confirmation B).[30] This confirmation is *in no sense* a completion of baptism, but repre-

sents, as for Episcopalians baptized in infancy, the occasion of a mature commitment to Christ in the presence
of a representative of the universal church; and it provides renewing of the Spirit through prayer and the laying on of hands.

(e) If adults baptized in another church have already
made a mature commitment to Christ in their former
denomination, *they should be received by the bishop.* The
appropriate manual act for the reception of new members from any denomination—whether Roman
Catholic, Orthodox, Lutheran, or Baptist—is the laying
on of hands, to symbolize that special link to the whole
church which our bishops represent to us. Such adults
also receive strengthening power of the Spirit through
prayer and the laying on of hands. The appropriate formula is that for Reception.[31]

(f) Confirmed adults—or those received from other
communions—who experience a deepening of faith to
which they wish to give public witness, may reaffirm
their baptismal vows before a bishop and receive the laying on of hands in blessing, with prayer for the Spirit.
This act may occur more than once.

(g) When laying on of hands is used in connection with
all three of these rites—Confirmation, Reception, and
Reaffirmation—it not only expresses a parallel and equal
prayer for renewal in each case, but has the further
advantage of securing the following desirable result: that
whether a person comes into the fellowship of the
Episcopal Church under the traditional interpretation of
the initiatory rite or under the interpretation suggested
in this paragraph, he or she will receive the episcopal
laying on of hands with prayers for the gift of the Spirit.

(h) The use of chrism in connection with the three rites
associated with Confirmation B is not appropriate.

19. The use of chrism at confirmation (i.e., Confirmation A) is ancient, and its symbolism complex. The biblical roots of the use of oil can be readily traced.[32] Oil represents the rich, flowing life of the Spirit.[33] It also suggests the anointing of the kingly and priestly people of God.[34] It lost its symbolic power for churches of the Reformation, including the English church. Its use was dropped in English and American Prayer Books after 1552.[35] Whether it will be generally regained under the present provision for optional use is uncertain. It is, in any case, improper to insist that it constitutes an *essential* symbol of the presence of the bishop at presbyteral baptism, when the priest lays a hand on the candidates and signs them with the sign of the cross. It may, of course, be taken to represent the bishop's presence in that action, since it can only be consecrated by a bishop. That level of meaning, however, was late to develop. Moreover, the presbyter on whom the bishop has laid hands at ordination is an even better symbol of the bishop's presence (because personal) than oil which the bishop has consecrated.

Although the use of oil may be regarded by some as enriching the initiatory rite, its use cannot be regarded as indispensable, nor may a baptism performed by a presbyter without chrism be regarded as incomplete.

NOTES

1. BCP, pp. 299-311. Cf. E.C. Whitaker, *Documents of the Baptismal Liturgy*, pp. 4-7 (Ap. Trad. of Hip.), pp. 142-147 (Ambrosian Manual), pp. 186-190 (Gelasian Sacramentary), p. 247 (Sarum Rite).

2. BCP 1928, p. 299. BCP 1549, Everyman's Library, London: J.M. Dent, 1910; p. 251. BCP 1552, ibid., p. 409. It is well known that the same rubric has appeared in every intervening English and American Prayer Book. The phrase "ready and desirous of being confirmed" was added in 1662 to accommodate both those who had not been confirmed during the

Commonwealth and those who lived in the new colonies. The mitigation implies that confirmation is not essential. In this case, it is maturity of faith which is required.

3. Cf. C.P. Price, *Liturgy for Living* (Seabury, 1979), pp. 103f.; Urban T. Holmes, *Young Children and the Eucharist* (Seabury, 1972).

4. Acts 8.36; 10.47; 16.33, among others. These are the clearest references.

5. *Didache* vii.1, 3.

6. Justin Martyr, I Apology 61.

7. Acts. 2.38; Matthew 28.19. Also *Didache* vii.1, 3; ix.5.

8. *Apostolic Tradition*, Part II, para. 21-23.

9. John 3.5; for sealing with the Spirit, cf. Ephesians 1.13.

10. I Peter 2.9.

11. Romans 6.34. Cf. Mark 8.34-35.

12. Matthew 28.19. This passage is cited as the institution of baptism by the risen Lord. It at least makes no explicit mention of liturgical actions in addition to water-baptism. In Jesus' own baptism, moreover, the coming of the Spirit, in the closest association with John's act ("straightway" according to St. Mark), involved no other liturgical act, but the sovereign freedom of the Spirit. For the essential unity of early baptismal liturgies, cf. G.W.H. Lampe, *Seal of the Spirit*, pp. 157f.

13. Alexander Schmemann, *Of Water and the Spirit*, passim. The whole book is an exposition of the rite of baptism in the Greek Orthodox Church.

14. Although bishops retained control of these ceremonies in western catholicism, they always could authorize priests to perform them. Only under Anglican discipline has confirmation been so rigorously maintained as a prerogative of bishops only. Cf. *New Catholic Encyclopedia*, vol. 4, p. 149 (b).

15. J.D.C. Fisher, *Bapt. in Med. West,* pp. 141ff; also, Lampe, *Seal of the Spirit,* p. 174; also, Fisher, *Confirmation Then and Now,* pp. 126-9.

16. Cf. Lampe, p. 179. Lampe places this development in the third century. It is one of the sacraments listed by Hugh of St. Victor (cf. B. Leeming, *Principles of Sacramental Theology* [Longmans, 1956], p. 566) and appears as one of the seven sacraments finally identified by Peter Lombard and Thomas Aquinas (*Summa Theologica* 3a.72).

17. Fisher, *Confirmation Then and Now,* pp. 127ff. The restriction of communion to those in danger of dying was soon lifted. Nevertheless, the question about the importance of confirmation continued to be asked. Cf. Fisher, *Christian Initiation: Baptism in the Medieval West,* pp. 20-21.

18. Fisher, *Bapt. in Med. West,* pp. 120-124.

19. E.g., Daniel B. Stevick, *Holy Baptism, Supplement* to PBS 26, p. 29.

20. Aquinas, *Summa Theologica* 3a.72.8.

21. J. Ridley, *Thomas Cranmer* (Clarendon Press, Oxford, 1962), p. 70.

22. Cf. *New Catholic Encyclopedia,* vol. 4, p. 149 (b); A. McCormack, *Christian Initiation,* p. 98. There are indications that even in Latin America, confirmation practice is coming to conform to that of the rest of western catholicism.

23. Cf. Whitaker, *Documents of the Baptismal Liturgy,* p. 188. Some scholars would place the origin of this prayer at an even earlier date. The phrase occurs in a prayer apparently used in this place in the liturgy discussed by St. Ambrose in *De Sacramentis* (4th century). Cf. Lampe, p. 208.

24. BCP 1979, pp. 420-1; *Services for Trial Use* (1970), pp. 326-7.

25. It would be a mistake to make too much of the earlier service of confirmation with the laying on of *a* hand, rather than the laying on *of hands*. In the Prayer Book tradition, the service of Confirmation had no subtitle until 1662, when *The Laying on of Hands* appeared. However the rubric directing the bishop's action involved a singular "hand" from 1549-1662. In American books, the subtitle *Laying on of Hands* was used in 1789, 1892, and 1928; the rubric was also in the plural in the first two American books. In 1979, the singular form "hand" goes with the end of baptism; the rubric in Confirmation B reads "hands." This fact may be taken as an indication of the revisers' intentions, although the point must not be pressed to the point of saying that Confirmation A, done with two hands, is somehow improper.

26. Canon Title I. 17.1(d), par. 2.

27. Cf. paragraph 17.

28. Canon Title I. 17.1(d), par. 1.

29. Canon Title I. 17.1(a).

30. Canon Title I. 17.1(c).

31. Canon title I. 17.1(d), par. 4.

32. Leonel L. Mitchell, *Baptismal Anointing* (SPCK, London, 1966).

33. E.g., Isaiah 61.1.

34. Revelation 1.6; Leviticus 8.10 (for priests); I Samuel 16.13 (for the messianic king of David's line).

35. Cf. BCP 1549, in *The First and Second Prayer Books of Edward VI*, Everyman's Library 448 (London: J.M. Dent & Sons, 1910), p. 241, connected with *baptism*. BCP 1552, in *The First and Second Prayer Books*, p. 398 (baptism), p. 408 (confirmation).

It is at least arguable that Cranmer intended the baptism liturgy of 1549 to be a reunited service. Not only was the use of oil directed in 1549, but the language of the prayer used at the consignation in the 1552 service of baptism—the language of the Christian soldier—is *confirmation* language, as

Marion Hatchett has argued in "The Rite of 'Confirmation' in The Book of Common Prayer and in *Authorized Services 1973," Anglican Theological Review 56* (1974): pp. 292-310. If Cranmer indeed intended to reunite baptism and confirmation, however, it must be acknowledged that the point was universally overlooked until the present round of revisions.

BIBLIOGRAPHY

These are a few of the books which have been influential in shaping the discussion which lies behind this paper:

Dix, Gregory. *The Theology of Confirmation in Relation to Baptism.* Dacre Press, Westminster, 1946.

A brief statement of the position identified in this paper as traditional.

Fisher, J.D.C. *Christian Initiation: Baptism in the Medieval West.* SPCK, London, 1965.

—.*Christian Initiation: The Reformation Period.* SPCK, London, 1970.

—.*Confirmation Then and Now.* SPCK, London, 1978.

Three Alcuin Club monographs which survey this question with depth and a wealth of scholarly references.

Kavanagh, Aidan. *The Shape of Baptism: The Rite of Christian Initiation.* Pueblo, New York, 1978.

A Roman Catholic study in the light of Vatican II decisions.

Lampe, G.W.H. *The Seal of the Spirit.* 2nd ed., SPCK, London, 1967.

A thorough examination of the patristic development, whose conclusions tend to the revisionist position identified in this paper.

McCormack, Arthur. "Christian Initiation," *Twentieth Century Encyclopedia of Catholicism.* Hawthorne Books, New York, 1969.

Schmemann, Alexander. *Of Water and the Spirit.* St. Vladimir's Press, 1974.

An exposition of the Greek Orthodox rite of initiation.

Stevick, Daniel B. *Holy Baptism, together with A Form for the Affirmation of Baptismal Vows with the Laying-on of Hands by the Bishop, also called Confirmation,* Supplement to Prayer Book Studies 26. Church Hymnal Corporation, New York, 1973. Revised edition: *Baptismal Moments; Baptismal Meanings.* Church Hymnal Corporation, New York, 1987.

An historical and theological exposition of the rite of initiation as proposed by the Standing Liturgical Commission in 1973.

Thornton, Lionel. *Confirmation, Its Place in the Baptismal Mystery.* Dacre Press, Westminster, 1954.

An ampler study than Dix's, from roughly the same point of view.

Whitaker, E.C., ed. *Documents of the Baptismal Liturgy,* 2nd ed. SPCK, London, 1970.

This useful volume contains original texts concerning baptism—liturgical, canonical, theological—from the Didache *to the Sarum Rite.*